$47.62

Under the Headset
Surviving Dispatcher Stress

Richard Behr

STAGGS
PUBLISHING

Under the Headset
Surviving Dispatcher Stress

By Richard Behr

Published by:

 Staggs Publishing
P.O. Box 890069
Temecula, CA 92589-0069 U.S.A.

http://www.staggspublishing.com

ISBN 0-9661970-4-6
First Printing 2000
Printed in the United States of America

For every person who has ever worn the headset
and every person that will wear the headset to
become a part of the noble profession of...

The Dispatcher

Acknowledgments

There are some very special people I would like to thank that helped me get to the point that I am at today. First of all, if it were not for Janet Childs and her very special, wonderful way of caring and teaching, I don't know if I would have survived CIS. When you speak of someone with a good heart, the definition rests within her; when you speak of a caring presence, you need look no further. Secondly, I would like to thank Kevin Willett for not only the opportunity to attend Janet's stress management classes and help with my healing process, but also for the opportunity for me to teach other dispatchers about CIS. His friendship, his caring, his concern, and his laughter have sealed a bond of brotherhood between us. To Sharon C. for her insights, our many discussions regarding CIS, and her friendship through some tough times.

To Sharon G. for her continued support and enthusiasm when it comes to teamwork. I also have to thank two police officer buddies of mine: Wayne and John. They supported me with their endeavors to learn and to be trained in debriefing techniques. Also for their professional as well as personal friendship and for making me laugh.

A special thank you to Kurt, Cindy, Judy and Les for the opportunity to spread the word to others that there is hope out there for dispatchers.

A very special thank you to Jan for her assistance with this project and her honesty. And to her "cohort in crime," Nancy. Both are special friends and a lot of fun to be with at conferences and, especially, a personal guided tour of their home state, Iowa.

To the instructors at Public Safety Training Consultants: Randall for his guidance and assistance in my endeavor, Dave for his insight and humor, Twonya for her kindness and her expression of love of others, Cindy for her patience and knowledge when I ask the same questions over and over and a shoulder to lean on, Tracy for her kindness and warped sense of humor, Karen for her warmth and ability to make others comfortable, Carol for her warmth and kindness, and Dr. Steve "Blind Melon" Dolezal for his different perspective of humor. They are no doubt, the worlds best dispatchers and dispatch instructors; but most importantly, they are friends.

To my former colleagues at SBPD who put up with me while I was in the midst of my critical incident: a thank you to Mike F., Mike B., Leo, Paul, Cheri, Al, Pam, Dena, Bob and Dodie and the rest of the dispatch crew. A special thanks to Ricki for her friendship and all the laughter. It was my mission in life to get her to laugh on the radio. Mission accomplished.

I would be remiss if I didn't give a thanks to those in my communications center. They work my hours when I'm out on the road teaching and don't complain about it. And to Administration for allowing me the opportunity to travel and to teach and all the encouragement they give me.

And most of all, my daughter who I don't think realizes what an inspiration she is to me. It was her that I thought of when under stress and the way she has always pronounced the word, "Daddy."

About the Author

Richard Behr has been in public safety for over 27 years. After a stint in the U.S. Navy as a photographer, his first job was with a private ambulance service. Richard then switched careers to become a firefighter. After 13 years he became a public safety dispatcher. During his career, Richard has received numerous commendations, letters of appreciation and has received his agency's Meritorious Service Medal and Medal of Bravery. He is a Member with Diplomate status of The American Academy of Experts in Traumatic Stress, is a Board Certified Expert in Traumatic Stress and is Board Certified in Emergency Crisis Response. He is a senior instructor for Public Safety Training Consultants, holds the position of adjunct instructor with Riverside Community College (CA) and teaches at Riverside County (CA) Sheriff's Department Ben Clark Training Center. He is Past Secretary and currently is the Vice President of Riverside County Law Enforcement Trainers Association (CA). Richard has been a presenter for several conferences around the country, including Associated Public Safety Officials (APCO) International and Regional Conferences and National Emergency Number Association (NENA) conferences. As a founding member of a critical incident stress debriefing (CISD) team, he has taught hundreds of dispatchers about the effects stress has on their job performance and personal lives.

Richard welcomes your questions and comments and can be contacted via E-Mail at **Richard@pstc911.com**

Table of Contents

A Personal Journey

I couldn't write a book about the stressors of being a dispatcher without having been through the critical incident stress nightmare itself. For those who have never experienced the effects of having to deal with a critical incident, it is very difficult to convey the feelings and emotions one may experience. And those who have been down that dark path and survived, smile and know what words cannot necessarily describe. So begins the story of my journey.

Clue. In law enforcement, we call it a clue. Being a police dispatcher is a stressful job. I had no clue. I was a Vietnam veteran and a veteran of 13 years in the fire service and EMS. I thought I had seen and dealt with everything there was to deal with. I had never heard of Critical Incident Stress let alone understand Post Traumatic Stress Syndrome. I didn't feel I had suffered any ill affects from the entire trauma I had witnessed over the years. Why did one particular incident have such a dramatic affect on me? Why had it taken all of those years to manifest itself? "Why" was becoming a "buzz" word in my vocabulary.

It started off a relatively mundane shift three days before Christmas. I was a rookie dispatcher working on being qualified on the primary radio channel. I had already been qualified answering 9-1-1 and business lines and qualified on the service desk and administrative radio channel. The swing shift was just starting and there were approximately 50 to 60 officers on the street. Calls were coming in and I was dispatching them almost the same time that they were entered into the computer aided dispatch. In fact, I started feeling pretty cocky about myself as I dispatched the calls in a timely manner. A call was received about a domestic disturbance between a man and wife who were arguing. This was nothing unusual around the holidays. The call stated that there may be weapons in the house, but it was unknown for sure. Two units were dispatched to the call and arrived a few minutes later. Shortly thereafter, they advised that they were Code 4; meaning O.K. in police jargon. Other calls continued to come in to the communications center and were being dispatched in a timely manner. A few minutes later, through the radio traffic of several officers trying to talk at once, I picked out a voice calling for emergency traffic. The frequency was cleared. An officer advised that both he and his partner were shot and his partner wasn't moving. Hesitantly swinging into action, I had one unit available to be dispatched as all other units were on calls and the oncoming shift was in briefing. The available unit was dispatched and medical aid was sent to a staging area until the area was secured. The shooting involved the officers on the domestic disturbance call.

I didn't know it at the time, but the call takers started receiving calls on 9-1-1 about the shooting before the officers called out the shooting a second time. A second call for help - that's the call I heard through all the radio traffic. I don't profess to know all about the technical side of radios. In fact, all I'm mainly concerned about is when I key up, I see the digital view meter moving and my voice goes out. By the same token, when the field units key up, I want to be able to hear their voices. We didn't find out until several days after the shooting, but there was a problem with the voice relay to our headsets. The best that I can explain it is this: when the voice from the field units comes in, it goes to the tape first and then is relayed to the headsets. A computer board had failed. I didn't hear their first call for help and neither did my trainer or anyone else in the center. It finally dawned on us that we had been asking the units to repeat themselves over and over for several days before the shooting. In fact, I had just chalked it up to sun spots, poor repeater locations or pure radio magic. I never thought a second thing about the officers getting upset over having to repeat themselves several times.

That was not the only time Mr. Murphy invited himself to this call. The second time occurred when, with only one unit available and responding, I heard 6 motor officers arrive on scene. I looked at the CAD screen and they weren't even logged on duty. Being that it was Christmas time, the motor units were out escorting Santa Claus around town while Santa passed out candy from the top of a fire engine. Much to my surprise, no one had informed us that these units would be out there. We were fortunate that they were in the area of the shooting and were first on scene. Mr. Murphy showed himself again when my trainer, who was sitting at the supervisor's console, tried to take over the call and realized that he couldn't. The radio foot pedal quit working at his position. He scrambled over to my position and plugged in his headset. Throughout the call, we both talked while I typed anything and everything I could into the incident screen.

It seemed like 10 minutes had passed until the crime scene was secured. Both officers, a civilian bystander and the suspect were transported to the hospital for gunshot wounds. In reality, forty-five minutes had passed since the initial call for officers down. While the incident was in progress, I looked up at my trainer and told him that after this was all over, I wanted a break from the radio. He told me I didn't have much choice, as it was always departmental policy to relieve the radio dispatcher after an officer involved shooting. Later, I was relieved from the radio and was told to spend as much time as I needed in the break room. If I decided to return to the communications room, I could work radio, phones or the service desk. After downing several soft drinks, I opted to return to the radio, climbing back on the proverbial horse. After an hour on the radio, my kidneys informed me that they needed a break. I asked to be relieved from the radio again. As I stood to unplug my headset, I began to uncontrollably shake. It lasted for a couple of hours but gradually subsided. In the mean time, my bladder felt like it was the size of a golf ball, so camping out in the restroom became crucial.

I placed a call to my girlfriend and told her what had happened. I explained that I didn't think I was doing very well with the situation. I went home at end of shift and explained to her what I was feeling. The two glasses of wine seemed to help. Sleep did not come easy that night or for a few nights afterwards. As I was to find out in the coming weeks, there were a lot of things that would not come easy.

The night of the shooting, the Chief, Assistant Chief, two Captains, a Sergeant and a counselor talked to all those who were involved with the shooting incident. The counselor told us that if we felt like we needed to talk, we should make an appointment with his office and come in for a one-on-one session. I felt I needed to talk to someone to see if I could find out what was bothering me about this particular incident. I made the call and went in to talk to him. As my posterior was settling into the chair, he told me he didn't know anything about my job and what the job entailed. My first thought was, "Well, if you don't know what it's all about, how are you going to relate to me?" I only lasted one more session before I decided that his time and mine was being wasted.

Going to work became harder and harder every day. It was during this time that I began to experience a gamut of emotions; a lot of them I wasn't aware I was capable of feeling. I felt anger. I was angry at the call taker who took the call as I felt they should have asked more questions to draw out the danger of the call. I was angry at the officers for, in my mind, not exercising more care. I was angry at myself for sending them on the call. Survivor's guilt set in; they wouldn't have been shot if I hadn't sent them on the call. Fear was a big emotional factor. I was afraid that I had made a mistake in the dispatch that contributed to the shooting. If the officers survived, I feared that they would blame me for dispatching them to the call. I didn't even know the officers, as our communications center was located in the basement of a building other than the police department. Officers rarely came down to visit the dungeon. To this day, I can't even begin to explain the emotions I went through. Some of them came and went very quickly and some stayed for months.

During the next two months, I had a fear of working the radio. I made every excuse I could think of so that I didn't have to go back on the radio. The thought of having a repeat situation terrified me. While driving to work, I formulated excuses as to why I couldn't work radio. Once I walked in the back door and walked down that long corridor to communications, it would feel like an earthquake in my guts. Gradually, I felt that I was learning to cope with the stress.

An opportunity arose to apply for another department-one with less radio traffic, fewer calls for service, and more importantly, less stress. It also offered better wages and benefits. I jumped at the opportunity and was hired. Shortly into my new dispatch position two events occurred. The pressure of the stress I was holding inside ruined the relationship I was in and sadly we parted ways. I felt remorse for the relationship, but I couldn't continue to put her through my personal hell. The second event was being placed in the position of coordinating training for communications personnel. These two changes that would turn my life around.

I was sent to a communications training officer class where, among other thing, we learned techniques of adult learning, legal aspects of training, stress management and so on. On the morning of our stress management block most of the class, including me, were suffering from the aftermath of a party the night before. I nudged the person setting next to me and told them to please wake me if anything important was discussed. The instructor walked in. She was a short petite woman with medium length blonde wavy hair, wearing a yellow sundress and sandals and carrying a guitar. My first impression was that she was a left over from the 60's and I thought, "Oh my goodness, we're going to hold hands and sing Kumbiya." As the class progressed, I thought I heard a four letter word come out of her mouth. I asked the person next to me if I had heard correctly. "Affirmative" was the answer. I figured that maybe she had something important to say and I had better pay attention. A few moments later, another swear word. The instructor asked the class if it offended them to hear four letter words. Before anyone could answer, she stated that if we were offended by profanity, we were in the wrong business. Throughout our career we were going to hear all kinds of four-letter words and be placed in situations that would cause stress. If we didn't learn to manage stress it could surely kill us. Needless to say, she had my undivided attention.

As the class progressed, I felt as if the instructor was talking directly to me and knew everything that I was feeling. I wondered whether she was psychic because she knew exactly what I was going through. She knew that I had trouble sleeping; trouble dealing with the stress of the job; had gone through a relationship problem with the eventual death of that relationship; had constant thoughts about the shooting incident, such as what did I do wrong, where did I go wrong, and it was all my fault because I was the one who sent the officers on the call. She knew the whole gamut of emotions that I had, and was still going through. I felt somewhat relieved that there was finally someone who understood. The pressure relief valve was finally opened.

I talked with the instructor after the class. To my delight, I found out that she and one of the other instructors provided classes on critical incident stress management and debriefing. I asked how I could attend a class and how soon. I felt the need to explore my feelings and this seemed the perfect opportunity. I was contacted a month later about hosting a class in stress management, and with my department's blessing, I did. To my amazement, 34 dispatchers had signed up for the class. During the class I discovered I was not alone in my feelings. Most importantly, I found out that I was normal and was having normal reactions to an abnormal situation. Yes! There was the light at the end of the tunnel. The instructor was Janet Childs.

To say that I thirsted for more knowledge would definitely be an understatement. An eight hour class explained the who, what, when, where, and why, but I needed more. Eventually, I attended additional courses on stress management and the debriefing process. In all, I've had in excess of 100 hours of training on CISD and CISM. I read everything I could get my hands on relating to law enforcement stress. I've attended seminars and researched whatever I could find. To my dismay, there was very little information on the affects of stress on dispatchers. I found some very good articles, but I could not find any statistics or studies of any kind that dealt with communications personnel. It seemed that dispatchers were the silent victims of CIS. Most dispatchers feel that they are second class citizens within the department, which is a source of stress in itself. They feel that most officers, supervision and administration have no clue as to what the job entails. This is most intriguing for an occupation that deals in clues. I felt I had to contribute in some small way to let dispatchers know that the effects of CIS are normal and their emotions and reactions are normal. In addition, no dispatcher should go through that roller coaster ride without an understanding of stress and what it can do. He or she can then be presented with tools and techniques to cope with the stress. Nothing is going to change the fact that stress will affect us in some way, but how we deal with the stress will affect our reaction to a stressful event. In other words, we can't change the action of the incident, but we can change our reaction to the incident. And the most important way one can do this is by pre-incident education and training.

On my journey through the effects of CIS and being a survivor of CIS, I realized several important factors. First, we are not alone in our feelings. There are a lot of dispatchers out there who are wounded puppies and, sadly, some don't even know it. Some feel that they don't suffer any stress from the job, and that may be true. Perhaps they have a great system of beliefs and a terrific support system or, simply that they know how to deal with stress. But for the majority that stress affects, there is help out there. And it doesn't have to be a walk through a maze to find it. Fortunately, there have been programs around for 20 years or more. Administrators are slowly discovering the ways to take care of the members of their respective departments, whether it be through a Mitchell model CIS program, Emergency Assistance Programs (EAP's), in-house psychological programs or educational programs.

I realized that I can contribute to the education of others. I could share my knowledge and experience about cumulative, occupational and critical incident stress; put into action the tools and techniques for coping and let other dispatchers know, as they said in the Mel Brooks movie "Young Frankenstein," that they weren't "Abby some-thing...Abby normal." I began teaching stress management to new and experienced dispatchers at a local sheriff's academy. I searched out other dispatchers that had been through critical incidents to form a local volunteer, non-profit CISD team. We have sent dis-patchers to CIS training, developed flyers for distribution and presented CIS concepts to agencies in three large Southern Califor-nia counties. Our feeling is that you don't have to be a member of our team or get involved with the team, but if they get the training and education, they should pass it on to others.

There was one interesting thing that I learned about the internal "earthquake" I would experience while walking down that long corridor to the communications center. The janitors had waxed the floor in the break room on the day of the shooting, and subcon-sciously I had associated that smell with the incident. So, every time I reported for duty I would smell that wax in the hallway and immediately begin to relive the trauma. With all of my CIS training and the teaching I have done, I can now state that I can safely wax my floors again without the fear of dealing with the Richter scale. Society has taught men that it is not manly to show affection and emotions, that men have to hide those feelings or be seen as being weak. Well, sometimes it takes a journey through hell to realize that the best way to deal with unexplored feelings, is to confront them head on. As the saying goes,"That which does not destroy me makes me stronger." As with anything new and unexplored, taking that first step into the unknown, especially when it may be dark in there, is the most frightening step of all. Light that candle of your being with education, knowledge and training and your steps will be well lit along life's path. Hopefully, this book will be your match with which to light that candle.

Oh, and by the way, to satisfy the curiosity that we as dispatchers feel; both officers survived as did the innocent civilian and the suspect. One officer returned to work a few weeks after the shoot-ing, but the other officer didn't come back until about a year later. I had spoken on the phone with the first returning officer and was relieved when he thanked me for what I did that day. A couple of years later, I had attended a charity football game between my former agency and another department. As I was sitting there, a friend of mine pointed out Mark. I asked, "Who's Mark?" He said, "You know, one of the officers that was shot while you were on the radio. Let's go talk to him." Immediately, my heart began to race and I felt the fear again of being blamed. My friend talked me into going over to meet to him. When I was introduced to him, he shook my hand vigorously, smiled and thanked me for what I did that day. All I can remember is that his hand seemed twice as large as mine. The feeling that came over me? The incident was finally put to rest.

The Boring Chapter
Or the stress process

Most dispatchers are action oriented and will take little time to read lengthy, boring material. Hence, the title of this chapter. However, it is important to understand the process that happens to us when we are under stress and I will attempt to explain the process in simple and concise terms.

Dispatchers work in a stressful environment. The same stressors are there for all of us, whether the agency you work for handles thirty 9-1-1 calls a shift or three hundred and whether you have 5 officers in the field or 100. It is the affects of these stressors that are manifest in our job and personal lives. To understand the stress process helps us understand how to cope with that stress.

Stress can be defined as **"mental or physical strain resulting from anxiety, work, or adjustive demands or challenges."** Does that sound like your job? As dispatchers, we are faced with many demands and challenges. Stressors are a large part of our job. A stressor is **"something capable of causing stress."** It can be the R/Ps (reporting party), the officers or firefighters in the field or just about anything we encounter during the shift.

A certain amount of stress is good for you. In fact, we need stress to function in our daily activities. This is called **eustress**, defined as **"the condition of heightened energy and optimal energy level for maximum performance."** This is the stress we need to survive. The "bad" stress or **distress** is that stress that has long term effects. **Distress "occurs when the stress level goes beyond optimum and overtaxes the physical, mental and emotional systems."** Stress implies a response and Hans Selye called it **The General Adaptive Syndrome.** It is the internal sequence of events that takes place in response to stress.

Simply put, the following is that sequence of events:

Stressor. The event that sets the sequence into motion. It may be that one phone call or the radio call for help that triggers the sequence.

Alarm Reaction. This is the "Fight or Flight" reaction. It is where we make that split second decision to react one way or another. If we go into the "fight" mode we prepare ourselves to meet the challenge and go into the...

Resistance Stage. If we successfully adapt, we build our confidence, feel more secure, develop strength, build our ability to cope and have greater resistance to additional stress.

However, if we do not successfully adapt, we go into the...

Exhaustion Stage. This stage can be dangerous over a period of time. It causes wear and tear on our internal systems. We can become weak from a depressed immune system, become more vulnerable to additional stress, our internal systems start to break down and it can eventually lead to death.

Biochemical/Physiological Affects

Keep in mind that this process happens within a split second. We don't have much say in what happens during this process. However, you can learn to help control it and cope with it. The following is a brief synopsis of what goes on inside our bodies when that stressor hits us:

1. Stressor

2. The Reticular Activating System sends an alarm message via the nerve system to the cerebral cortex. There it interprets the signal as danger.

3. The cerebral cortex sends a message to the adrenal glands to produce epinephrine, better known as adrenaline, and dump it into the blood stream. This causes the body to go into the "fight or flight" mode. There is an increase in the heart rate, blood pressure, accompanied with rapid breathing; the blood vessels dilate sending blood to the vital organs; blood is taken away from the skin and digestive track. We begin to develop tunnel vision and selective hearing.

4. About 20-30 minutes later, Aldosterone is released into the blood stream. Aldosterone promotes water retention and keeps the blood pressure elevated.

5. Cortisol is released several hours after the stressor. This inhibits the production of killer T-cells. Killer T-cells help kill the bodies invaders and ward off infection and diseases. Cortisol allows the body to convert sugar to energy more effectively. It's elevation is responsible for states ranging from acute awareness to panic.

6. Finally, the body releases endorphins that help numb the body and take away pain.

All of these responses have helped us survive all of these years. From our early ancestors who had to hunt for food, these responses served us well. Predators when they hunt, always put themselves at risk for injury. Man always did until they invented ways to distance themselves from their prey and the risk of injury. Up until the invention of the spear, bow and arrow and finally the gun, man was always at risk when hunting for food. These body responses helped to minimize any injury encountered. The tunnel vision helped focus on the task at hand; mainly the prey. The elevated heart rate, blood pressure and breathing rate kept oxygen flowing to the vital organs. Blood leaving the skin and digestive system helped reduce bleeding in case of injury. After all, when trying to run down and kill a prey, you didn't need the stomach or intestines until after the kill.

Now we need to look at the downside of these responses. Over a prolonged period of time, all of these chemicals that are dumped into our bodies can cause us harm.

1. **Epinephrine** can cause gas, pain and nausea. The skin turns cyanotic or a bluish in color. The heart rate remains elevated, making us prone to heart disease. High blood pressure or hypertension can develop and lead to kidney disease. We experience mood swings, which can cause us emotional or physical problems and lead to relationship problems with our co-workers or loved ones. Finally, we can develop irritable bowel syndrome.

2. **Aldosterone** kills kidney cells and promotes hypertension.

3. **Cortisol** suppresses the immune system, produces ulcers and causes the skin to thin out and tear easily.

Dispatchers are faced with several types of stress that are all contributing factors to the stress level. And after all the bad news, don't we just want to know what those other types of stress are?

1. **Delayed** stress is that stress we bury inside ourselves over a period of time. We haven't effectively dealt with a situation and we tend to hide it within ourselves.

2. **Cumulative** stress comes from all different sources. It could be trouble paying the bills, health problems, worrying about paying for your child's higher education and so forth. It's a variety of stressors coming at you from all angles.

3. **Occupational** stress is the job itself. Dispatching and stress go hand in hand. Dispatching is a stressful job!

4. **CIS or Critical Incident Stress** is that one particular incident that overwhelms our ability to cope. It may be that caller's voice that reminds you of your dearly departed grandmother, the baby drowning call, or the officer or firefighter killed or injured in the line of duty. However, it doesn't even have to be one of those high priority calls to cause the stress response. It can be something very simple that elicits your reaction. CISM (Critical Incident Stress Management) is the process of managing Critical Incident Stress.

The Boiling Frog

If we liken ourselves to a frog and our job and work environment to a pan of water, it may help illustrate the affect of stress on our body. If we place a frog in a pan of cold water then place that pan on top of the burner, the frog eventually becomes used to the water and adapts to the temperature. If we turn the burner on simmer the water heats up, the frog becomes used to the water and adapts to the temperature. If we then turn up the heat to medium, the water becomes hotter, the frog becomes used to the water and adapts to the temperature. If we then turn the burner to high, the water will eventually boil, and the frog becomes used to the water and starts to adapt to the temperature. What happens to the frog? It eventually dies. The more stress we are subject to, the more we become used to it and adapt. If we don't do anything about the heat, we too can succumb to the boiling water of stress.

Signs and Symptoms of Stress

Physical	Cognitive	Emotional	Behavioral
Chills	Confusion	Fear	Withdrawal
Thirst	Nightmares	Guilt	Antisocial
Fatigue	Uncertainty	Grief	Inability to rest
Fainting	Suspiciousness	Denial	Erratic behavior
Dizziness	blames others	Agitation	Changes speech/words
Chest pain	Disorientation	Depression	Appetite changes
Headaches	Short term memory	Intense anger	Hyper alertness
Elevated BP	loss	Emotional shock	Alcohol problems
Rapid heart rate	Flashbacks	Helplessness	Aggression
Uncontrolled sweating	Time line distortion	Despair	Hostile
Shortness of breathe		Anger	
Tunnel vision		Sadness	
Shakiness			
Nausea/Vomiting			
Body tension			

These signs and symptoms are only the tip of the iceberg, but they are some of the most prominent signs that can manifest themselves during and after a critical incident. There are some internet web sites listed at the end of this book for those wanting to read more about signs and symptoms of stress.

Stress Health Facts

- A law enforcement officer's life expectancy is 57.8 years compared to 75 years for the general population.

- 58 to 62% of police officers take antacids.

- Angina (chest pain) is experienced by 39% of officers.

- Officers have a 1.7 times greater chance of developing cancer.

- Women who do not exercise have a 50% greater chance of developing breast, uterine or ovarian cancer.

- Only 28 to 32% of officers reach normal service retirement.

These statistics were taken from the October 1997 issue of Roll Call Training Bulletin. **Hey, what about us dispatchers?** Unfortunately, I haven't been able to find any statistics regarding dispatcher health facts. The good news is that there is a dispatcher who is collecting health data on dispatchers for a thesis. When that data becomes available, hopefully we'll be able to publish those facts in future editions.

Emergency Services Personality Profile

To better understand why stress affects us, we have to understand our personality traits. Just about every dispatcher, firefighter, police officer, EMT and paramedic, and others in the emergency service field, are what is called, "Type A" personality. In fact, most of us could be classified an "A Plus." According to Guy Schiller of the International Critical Incident Stress Foundation, "Law enforcement is one of the very few professions that drastically change a personality." When we began our careers as dispatchers, some of us may have had culture shock during our first few months of training. We weren't prepared for what we were going to encounter on the job. After a few years, we tend to become hardened to the things we are exposed to day in and day out. We can even become a little apathetic towards our fellow human beings. It's a natural process and is a defense mechanism to protect our emotions from the tragedy and problems we encounter during work. After all, rarely does someone call 9-1-1 to tell us that we are doing a great job. This generally only happens after an incident such as the Columbine High School shooting has thrust a communications center into the national spotlight. As of this writing, the members of the Jefferson County Sheriff and Littleton Fire Department communications centers are still receiving praise for the exceptional way they handled that tragic incident.

Here are some of the personality traits we exhibit as dispatchers.

1. **Obsessive / Compulsive.** It doesn't mean to the point of being neurotic; instead, it just means that we want things done right the first time, every time.

2. **Controllers.** Dispatchers are controlling people. We control the incident from the first phone call to the end of the incident. If things get out of control, we tend to panic a little. We also extend this need for control into our personal lives.

3. **Action oriented.** We like the action this job can bring. Why? Part of it is the adrenaline rush. Adrenaline is a drug and it is as addictive as alcohol, tobacco or drugs. It helps keep our baseline stress level above that of the average population.

4. **Easily bored.** Oh yeah, we can't just sit around and do nothing. It is especially hard for those on graveyard shift when there is nothing going on. The streets are dead and there is nothing moving for the officers to affect traffic stops. Usually fire and EMS agencies have plenty to do on the graveyard shift. It seems a lot of heart attacks, strokes, and those citizens who have the bad cold and wait until the stroke of midnight to call for help rather than seeing their doctor during daylight hours.

5. **High need for stimulation.** We have to have our minds and hands doing something. For those that are "yard dogs" (grave- yards), this is especially true. If it's slow, we need something to do.

6. **Risk takers.** Emergency service workers will take risks; not those that will cause us harm, necessarily, but we like to live on the edge of the envelope sometimes. That's why a lot of police officers have those boats, motorcycles, and other toys that give them an adrenaline rush when they're off duty. We have that need to keep that rush going, even on our off time. One defini- tion of a California police officer is: "divorced boat owner."

7. **Highly dedicated.** You bet! We may not the like the politics of the job or agency where we work, but if any outsider bad mouths our department or co-workers, we're one of the first to stand and defend. Some dispatchers even go as far as to say they love their job. It's okay to "luv" your job, but if you "love" your job, you set yourself up with an intimate relationship with your job. If problems arise in that job relationship, it has the same affect on us as a personal relationship. Think about a line in the movie "Trains, Planes and Automobiles." John Candy's character tells Steve Martin's character to, "Like your job, love your family and friends." Don't put the job before your family and friends.

8. **Strong need to be needed.** It gives us a sense of worth when people call us for help or to solve their problem for them. It makes us feel good. I haven't met a dispatcher yet who hasn't felt good about saving a life performing EMD, helping catch that robbery suspect, or searching data bases and finding the real name of that suspect that you knew was lying to your officer.

9. **Difficulty saying no.** We will sometimes schedule more activities, projects and errands into our day than we have time. It's just that we don't want to disappoint others.

10. **Rescue personality.** Dispatchers want to make things better. Believe it or not, that's one reason why we got into this line of work in the first place. We want to help take that problem away. This is especially true of us guys. We want to "fix" things and make it better.

11. **Family oriented.** Big time. This does not only include our immediate family, but also our law enforcement family. Sometimes we will put the law enforcement family ahead of our own. Like all families, we will argue and bicker with our co-workers, but when the stuff hits the proverbial fan, we pull together, work together and will defend one another.

12. **Driven by internal motivation.** We can be our own worst enemy when things go wrong. We second guess ourselves with "I should have done..." We are proud of what we do, which in turn makes us want to better ourselves.

13. **General high tolerance of stress**. It's part of our personality and we have been developing our personality all our lives. So if we are a "type A", we have been generally dealing with life's stressors all along.

According to Drs. Meyer Friedman and Ray Rosenman, there are a few more things to take into consideration when assessing ourselves:

Failing to stop and smell the roses

Hurrying the speech of others

Becoming unduly irritated when forced to wait in line or driving behind a car that is going too slow

Explosive speech patterns or frequent use of obscenities

Always having to be on time

Competitiveness and playing nearly every game to win

Measuring success in terms of numbers

Knee-jiggling or rapid finger tapping

I see a red flag when dispatchers start bragging about how many calls they answered or dispatched during their shift. It tends to make the quality of customer service decline in the sake of "keeping up with the Jones's" and showing that you can handle the calls with the best of them. Another trait is becoming impatient when watching others do things you can do better. This is especially true of trainers. One of the hardest things to do with trainees is to sit back and let them do things at their pace. We make facial and body contortions, clinch our fists, grunt and groan, sweat and mentally push them along until the task is completed. All of these or parts of these traits are who we are. They are our make up. They serve us in ways nothing could and, most of the time, it is done well. However, they can also be our Achilles tendon when not properly handled.

Identifying Our Stressors

An unknown author wrote, "Some people are like popcorn. You don't learn what they're really made of until you put heat under them." The heat that is placed under us is the stress we encounter every time we put on the headset. Let's try a little exercise to identify some of the stressors faced in the communications center. For now, let's not deal with call types, but those specific things that go on in our work environment and the things that affect us.

Take out a piece of paper and make a column with the following titles. If you need more paper, please do so.

> **Communications Center Manager**
> **Communications Supervisor**
> **Communications Training Supervisor**
> **Communications Training Officer**
> **Front line dispatcher**
> **Front line call taker**
> **Trainee**

If your agency doesn't use one or more of these specific titles, replace them with those you do utilize. If you have some that are not listed here, add those as well. Now list all of the things that you can think of that would be a stressor for each of these jobs. Here's one to help you get started: **the budget.** Below are some that have been suggested during classes and seminars. Try it yourself before referring to the list below.

Did you come up with some that aren't listed below? Are there some that you found are inherent to each position? Do you find that most of them are interchangeable? Are you finding you have a better appreciation for each individual position and that we all have certain job stressors?

1. **Status within the department.** Most dispatchers feel that they are second class citizens. This can be due, in part, to officers perpetuating "If you ain't sworn, you ain't born." Many fail to realize the fact that the dispatcher is the first on scene of any call. It's the dispatcher who obtains the initial information and keeps track of the officer's status, making sure they are safe once they are on scene. I know of some officers who get upset because the dispatcher has done a safety check on them. We know they are busy on scene, but we need to know that they are out of harm's way. I tell them I do it not for them, but for me; for my peace of mind and that of their beat partners. Another thing officers fail to realize is that we are their lifeline. If we

don't maintain contact with them, how will anyone know if they need assistance.

2. **Irregular breaks.** Most communications centers in this country have two or less dispatchers working per shift. This is frightening at times, especially if there is only one dispatcher on duty. How do you get to eat at the console? How do they get to go to the restroom without calling in a field officer, firefighter, or another civilian employee to cover the radio and phones? And as soon as you do, wouldn't you know it, Mr. Murphy shows up uninvited. Larger departments are more apt to have policy in effect that allows for a meal period and usually two or three break periods. But, it's not always the case for most dispatchers.

3. **Lack of control.** Remember our personality type? We are controlling people. We will even refuse to give up the radio on a long drawn out incident just so we can maintain that sense of control. Our perception is that it is our incident, we'll follow it through. What is the first thing we do when we answer that phone and start receiving information? Being aurally-oriented, we begin to visualize what is going on and the make up of the scene. It becomes our perception. How many of us have ever gone to the scene of an incident after it's all over, and find that it wasn't anything like you imagined? Especially if you weren't familiar with the area? **80% of the incident was perception, 20% was reality.** Something we have no control over and can only visualize can be a major stressor. Just ask a dispatcher who has handled an officer or firefighter down situation.

4. **Lack of recognition.** This and the next heading are probably one of the most important to dispatchers. They do work everyday that makes a difference in people's lives. Any dispatcher who has ever received a commendation, medal, or some other type of recognition, will tell you "I was just doing my job." We don't go looking for accolades, but when they are put upon us, we tend to down play our role and say anyone would have done the same. The role that was so very important. You've seen it on the news that an officer, firefighter, or involved citizen will say anyone would have done it, but we do it on a daily basis. However, the fact remains, we like to be recognized for a job well done and it makes us feel good. It validates us as dispatchers that we are doing the best job we know how to do.

5. **Lack of support.** Going hand in hand with lack of recognition is this topic. If we aren't being recognized for doing an outstanding job, we'll surely be recognized for making a mistake. Or perhaps you made a decision that was in the gray area and you're called on the carpet for it. Maybe there is no policy covering our actions, or possibly it could be that administration or supervision gives no support to the center in general. This could go back to status within the department itself.

6. **Dispatcher Sniper School.** No, this is not a special school dispatchers can attend. It is the habit of co-workers taking pot shots at co-workers, either under their breath or behind their intended victim's back. It can also be called Monday Morning Quarterbacking or 20/20 hindsight. Some dispatchers think they can always do the job better than the person who was in the hot seat. Well guess what? Their butt wasn't in the hot seat when the call went down, so realistically who knows how they would have reacted? Snide comments not only lead to poor morale, but can be hurtful and stressful, particularly if it's involving a critical incident.

7. **Equipment.** This can be antiquated as well as new equipment. We all have perfect radio systems with no dead spots, a CAD system that is so reliable that no "CAD has crashed" broadcast is ever made, headsets that are free of static and always work, chairs that are comfortable and even perform as advertised, lighting that is easy on the eyes without reflecting on the monitors, phone systems that work all the time without unaccountable disconnects, and a television set for local weather updates and for watching that pursuit coming into our area or the major incident we are working. No? Hmm, these problems seem to be somewhat universal, don't they?

8. **Administration.** This is especially a problem if a member of administration worked as a dispatcher in the past. We tend to think that they have forgotten what it was like to be in the trenches. Some administrators think that National Telecommunicator Week is also translated into Secretary's Day. They may not believe that dispatching is a profession.

9. **Lack of closure or blending.** This is especially true in larger agencies. We won't always know the outcome of an incident unless we look it up at the end of our shift or at the start of our next shift. If it's one of those calls that bothers us and we never know the outcome we don't get the closure you need. I personally don't like the term closure, I prefer the term that Sharon, a close friend of mine coined: blending. Closure connotes a closing; as in the closing of a door. That simply is not true. Because of the way our minds work, we will revisit or be reminded of the incident in the future. When we hear a favorite song, it reminds us of something in our life. Whether it was good or bad, we can remember what we were doing, or a special moment. If we think in terms of making a recipe, all of the ingredients are blend them together. Life is like that recipe; we blend all kinds of things into it to make the final product. If we take stress and blend it into our lives, the stress is still there as an ingredient, but it is diluted and blended in with every other facet of life.

10. **Shift work.** This can be very stressful to our bodies and Circadian rhythms. Some people like working graveyard shifts while others absolutely hate it. Personally, I can't sleep during the day as I get older. Once our bodies get used to a certain shift, bingo, we move to another shift and have to start the process all over again. After a few years, it can take a toll emotionally and physically. One trick is to maintain a normal schedule as possible regardless of which shift we are working. If working the graveyard shift, don't go right home and crawl into bed. We don't go right to bed when we're working the day shift, do we? Makes sense, doesn't it?

11. **Work environment.** This is a different problem from equipment, but the two are related. In the old days, the dispatcher sat at the front desk with the desk sergeant. Then they were moved into a back room. During the 1950's and 1960's the dispatcher was moved to the basement of a building, not necessarily the police department itself. This was due to the fear of a nuclear bomb destroying the communications center. Consequently, there are a lot of communications centers that are in the basements of buildings, perpetuating the dungeon or mushroom syndrome. One concern about being in the basement is the lack of windows. It's a sad statement when a dispatcher has to get on the radio and ask the field units for a weather update, or whether it's light or dark outside. Fortunately, as Bob Dylan sang a few decades ago, "The times they are a changing." Across the country there is a growing realization that the communications center needs to be on the first or second floor of the department. This promotes camaraderie among officers and dispatchers. They can now place the voice with a face. It helps do away with the "us vs. them." Some centers across the nation are consolidating several agencies into one dispatch. This is mainly due to monetary and budgetary issues. It's cheaper to maintain one center rather than several.

12. **Sedentary jobs.** For the most part, our job consists of sitting on our tush for eight, ten, or twelve hours a day with only our fingers, hands, eyes and jaws getting any exercise.

13. **Diets.** Do we not have the most atrocious diet? The dispatcher food groups are fat, sugar, grease, caffeine, and chocolate. Dispatchers, particularly those on graveyard shift, will usually eat fast food since that is usually the only type of place in town open after midnight.

14. **Expectations.** Our expectations can be a source of our stress. During the application process and oral interview, probably one of the questions asked was, "Why do you want to be a dispatcher?" And more than likely, we all responded something similar to, "I want to help and be of service to the community." Anyone who has sat on an oral board has heard this response in

one form or another. However, after a while, that feeling changes. We may have been thinking that we were going to do life saving work each and every day. It just doesn't happen that way, no matter what the reality-based TV shows air during prime time. Even though every day may bring different circumstances, it's the mundane, everyday calls that make us become a little hardened: those "frequent flyer" callers; the calls on 9-1-1 wanting information on anything from the weather report to the local bus schedule; the calls for the barking dog while you are working a major incident; and the callers wanting to know what time the power is going to come back on after a power outage. We receive them every day, all across the nation. And they can be stressful to us because we expect 9-1-1 calls to be a life threatening emergency. They can be stressful if we let them.

Specific Dispatch Stressors

Let's try another exercise. Take a piece of paper and list the types of calls that cause a stress response. Take another piece of paper and cover up the list below, then see how many of your choices match the list provided.

Types of Calls

Officer, firefighter, or medic killed or injured in the line of duty

Children killed or injured

Foot pursuits

Traffic pursuits

Felonies in progress

Prowler calls

Suspicious circumstances (especially those calls that we type code as suspicious circumstances when we aren't really sure what is going on)

Weapons calls

Domestic disputes

Traffic stops

Fighting in public

School shootings

Workplace violence

Sexual assault or rape

Robbery

Car jacking

Major disasters

SWAT operations

Long drawn out incidents

Multiple-casualty incidents
Any infrequent critical emergency involving numerous responders
EMD calls involving children or hysterical parents

Well, how did you do? When you stop to think about the number of call types that cause us stress, it's amazing what we deal with on a day-to-day basis. It boils down to the fact that in our profession we deal with the tragic circumstances. We deal with the suffering, property damage, the inhumanity people inflict on each other, the misguided, the unfortunate, the sociopath and so forth. It's no wonder that we can feel stressed by all that we encounter. And that's just on an aural level. Think about the stressors officers, deputies, firefighters, EMTs, and paramedics encounter when they have to function on an added level of the visual. Is it any wonder that they suffer from the same types of stress? It can be different, but it can be the same. Field personnel see and hear what goes on, while we can only visualize and come up with our own perceptions. And, remember, we are our own worst enemy, it is by no means our fault. It just becomes a matter of our job circumstances. We're inside, they're outside.

Ways to Cope with Stress

Well, now that we've explored the negative aspects of stress and looked at some of our stressors, let's move on to the good news. You can deflect the affects of stress and minimize the responses. Before we can move on, we need to understand something else about ourselves. There is a hierarchy about us that needs to be fulfilled before we can ultimately take care of ourselves. It's called Maslow's Hierarchy of Needs.

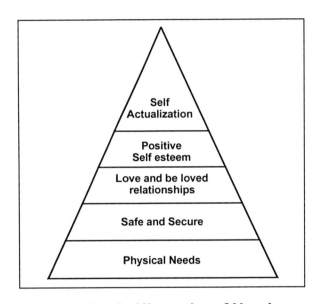

Maslow's Hierarchy of Needs

In a nutshell, the base of the pyramid requires that we have food, clothing and shelter. That meets our physical needs. Second, we need to feel safe and secure in our personal world. Third, we need to be in those relationships where we exchange love; our spouses, significant others, children, relatives, friends and yes, even our co-workers. Positive self-esteem means we feel good about ourselves and self-actualization is our meaning in life. If anyone of these levels fail, our whole pyramid can tumble down to the level of basic physical needs. This, of course is the extreme, which usually is the starting process of Post Traumatic Stress Disorder or PTSD.

What you need/don't need

Okay, it's time to grab another piece of paper. Draw a line down the center from the top of the page to the bottom. On the left column, write the label "Need." On the right column, write the label "Don't

Need." Now, visualize your self under stress. Write down things that you think you might need during stress. When you have finished, direct your attention to those things you think you don't need when under stress. Again, try it on your own before looking at the list below.

Need	**Don't Need**
Support	Monday Morning Quarter backing
Listening	Advise
Support system	Embarrassment
Physical safety	Humiliation
Honesty	Locked in a room by yourself
Acknowledgment	being ignored
Critical Incident Debriefing	dealing with nicknames
Food and sustenance	Clichés
Support from someone who has	"War" stories
lived through a critical incident	False assurance
Display of department support	minimizing the incident
Protection from the public and media	Abandoned by the department

Now that you've finished this list, there is one more I would like you to try. Instead of imagining you are under stress, imagine that someone who is near and dear to you has just passed away. Place yourself in the grieving process. When you have done that, try again to make a list of what you need and don't need on the back of your first list.

Are there any similarities between the two? There should be. Now comes the profound statement. **Stress knows no time line. Stress and grief are the same physiological and biological responses.** Our bodies don't know the difference, we just label them differently to make sense to us. We go through the same process of grieving as we do when under tremendous stress. Some responses may seem stronger at times than others, but it's basically all the same process. If you liken stress to cement and our lives as rubber wading boots, whenever the cement is shoveled inside the boots, if we don't get rid of the cement while it is wet, it will become more difficult to function as the cement hardens. Sure, there may be some residue cement left over, but it depends on how well we cope with that cement residue and the techniques we use to get rid of it that allow us to continue to function.

Let's address some of the things on the list you need.

Support — you definitely need the support of your family and peers. They form the core of our support system. They are the ones who know us inside and out. Our family members know us better than we do our self. Particularly when we are under stress; we don't always know what may be bothering us, but yet, it may be very plain to them.

Listening — someone to listen to what you have to say is important to us. Dispatchers are great listeners; it's part of our job. By being an active listener, you allow someone to release some of those pent up emotions. And sometimes, you don't even have to say anything other than helping validate what is being said.

Physical safety — going back to Maslow's Hierarchy of Needs, we need to have that safe and secure feeling. Safe from the trauma of the incident.

Honesty — we need honesty about the event and to have others be honest with us. After all, honesty is the best policy. If we don't have honesty, we will be subject to skepticism and start second-guessing ourselves.

CISD — Critical Incident Stress Debriefing. Why? Because it works when done properly. It gives us the opportunity to see that we are not alone in some of our feelings, that others are feeling similarities and going through similar experiences. It also helps us to adjust back into the stream of things and educates us. The process gives us the opportunity to express our feelings and emotions and bring them to the surface with the support of others in an atmosphere of trust and confidentiality.

Food and sustenance — under stress, our bodies become dehydrated and need to be refueled. You can become dehydrated when under stress.

Support from a survivor of a critical incident — it validates to us that the event is survivable. Someone else has experienced something similar and is now sitting there explaining what they felt during their incident.

Department support — it lets you know that you are not being abandoned by your agency, that they will support you in policy. This can be a major support system for you, the dispatcher, but officers as well. It shows that the department really does care about their family.

Protection from the public and media — the public doesn't understand police tactics so they are quick to condemn something that doesn't seem right to them. And the media can cause secondary trauma with their repeated "breaking news" that drags out for hours and even days. Not to mention if there is going to be a trial. As Gavin de Becker, a world renown expert on predicting violence stated at an emergency conference on school shootings, "Wouldn't you love to hear the media say the following, 'Next up on the news live at five, 40 minutes of nonsense and BS." The media can be a friend or a mortal foe. They can assist or hinder an investigation. When you are suffering the affects of a stressful incident, you don't need the speculation of the media and their second-guessing.

Some of the things you don't need:

Criticism — you did the best you could at that moment and after all, those doing the criticism didn't have their lower posterior in the hot seat at the time.

Advice — it's like noses, everyone has advice. It's up to you to choose what you listen to and what advise you'll heed. You don't need to hear someone say, "Well, I would have handled it this way..." Oh yeah, well here again, guess whose tush was in the hot seat.

Embarrassment — can be very damaging to our ego. If we are second guessing our actions, to begin with, we don't need to feel ashamed about our actions or have mistakes pointed out by others.

Humiliation — you may be feeling rotten over the incident anyway, you don't need to have your pride and self respect taken from you.

Locked in room alone — this gives a connotation that you did something wrong. Another reason officers don't need to be transported back to the station in the back seat of patrol unit after they shoot someone. It makes them feel like they did something wrong and are being treated like the folks who DO ride in the back of patrol units.

Dealing with nicknames — you don't want to hear nicknames like "killer" or "shooter." They only make you feel worse, so think about it before you attach a nickname to someone.

Clichés — one of the worst things you could say to someone is "It could have been worse." How could it have been worse? For you, it's probably the worst thing you have ever or will experience in your career!

"War" stories — if you hate sitting in a class where there is nothing but war stories, you feel cheated that you missed something of importance. War stories have their place and point, and can be beneficial to help you deal with the situation. It just has to be presented in a manner that is positive to the recipient and something to perhaps learn from.

Minimizing the incident — so what if a peer isn't affected by your incident. They may have dealt with something similar and coped very well. But by the same token, don't minimize another persons incident because it may be the most horrible experience they have been faced with. Not everyone is affected the same way. Try and remember the Rule of Thirds; one third of your center will not be affected by an incident, one third will be affected, and one third will be greatly affected and possibly suffer from CIS.

Abandoned by the department — this by itself can make you feel like you are on a deserted island and that your department isn't going to stand by you and support you.

Coping Techniques

They are a number of ways to cope with stress. I've only listed some of them below. As with anything, you will have to explore through a trial and error period to see what works best for you. Use the tools in your Dispatcher Tool Box.

1. **Preparation and education**. You are already preparing and educating yourself by reading this book. Dispatchers are resourceful people. For those who have access to the internet, try typing "critical incident stress" or "cis" into your search engine. You'll probably get over 20,000 hits. Find the ones pertaining law enforcement stress, many of them have topics related to dispatcher stress. If they don't and deal with officer stress, read them anyway. As stated in a previous section of this book, officer and dispatcher stress are very similar.

2. **Rational thinking**. Sometimes, when under stress, rational thinking goes right out the window. If we keep that inner dialogue going that tells us we're doing okay, we can keep our anchor point based in reality and in the here and now.

3. **Escape**. Take a break from the source of trauma. Get away! Don't wait until you are in burn out to take a vacation. Plan and take those vacations. Even if it's just a day or two to get away. Try taking a short 10 or 15-minute break from the radio or phones and talk with others about anything but the job. Spend a few moments in quiet. Think of a pleasant place you've been to and enjoyed. It's not called a mental vacation for nothing.

4. **Humor.** My favorite. We think we have the sickest humor in the world. Why? It's in part due to a defense mechanism. By making light of a situation, it's keeps a certain distance from our emotions. As long as the humor doesn't hurt anyone, it's okay to use humor. I was teaching a class and talking about a particular incident that happened on my shift one night. One of my buddies was coming back from dinner one night and happened to be coming to a freeway overpass when he saw something drop in front of his unit. He got out to check it out and discovered someone had jumped off the overpass. This was the first time he had encountered such a gruesome site. My friend was upset by the fact that he felt he could have done more for this person but didn't know what. After I let him talk out his emotions, I asked him what the silver lining was to this call. Now, I was teaching a stress management class one day and I asked this particular class the same question. In the back a dispatcher spoke up and said "At least he didn't land on the hood of the unit." Seems a little morbid, but the class broke out in laughter because we all understood those situations. All humor aside, the real answer was a somber, "At least he didn't die alone. Another

caring human being was with him at the end." Just remember this to help keep things in perspective. People mangled in traffic accidents are not FUBAR. People who die in fires are not "crispy critters." Don't dehumanize their death; they were living, feeling people. But use humor to lighten a situation as long as there is no harm done. It's been said that humor can be a two edged sword. Use the good edge to help you cope. Laughter really is the best medicine.

5. **Hobbies.** Another favorite of mine. If you don't have a hobby, get one! Whether it's working in the garden, elaborate vacations to exotic places, reading, sewing, fishing, going to sporting events, or collecting something, it takes your mind off what is bothering you and makes you focus on something you enjoy doing. Plus it helps relax you. Me, I collect toy fire trucks from all over the world. Take up a hobby or spend time with your hobby, it'll do you a world of good. As a bit of humor, remember, there can be a fine line between a hobby and mental illness.

6. **Take training classes**. It keeps you sharp at your profession, it introduces new ideas and concepts, keeps you updated and besides, it's good to get away once in a while. I know what you're thinking, there isn't money in the budget for training. It seems to be a common malady in public safety. Here's a thought, if you can afford it, pay for it yourself. Go to seminars and conferences, turn them into a vacation. I can think of two conferences to attend each year that only cost travel, hotel, registration and meals; the APCO international and NENA national conferences. Most chapters have state conferences as well. Plan to attend one. You can attend seminars and classes to learn more, as well as network with other dispatchers and interact with them. It's a great way to make new friends. A dispatcher friend of mine, Linda, takes a month vacation during the APCO international conference every year. She attends the conference, site sees and does some traveling. She has also met new friends, caught up with old friends, and even met those she corresponds with but hasn't met face to face. Check into it, a lot of dispatchers make it a family event.

7. **Training**. At your agency, do you train on a CAD system? Does your CAD system have a training mode to practice on? If you are a trainer, do you put your trainee through actual telephone and radio scenarios so that they don't look like the proverbial deer in the headlights once they are put on the phones or radio? Are you training in reality? To borrow and slightly change a military phrase; "Train like you work, and work like you train."

8. **Acknowledge.** By acknowledging the fact that you have a stressful job, you pave the way for understanding the affects of stress. Why do you think the first step of any step program is acknowledgment that there is a problem? You also need to acknowledge your feelings and emotions. When faced with an experience

that affects you, when you acknowledge those feelings, you bring them to the surface and can more readily deal with them.

9. **Talk it out**. The more you get those feelings out, the better equipped you are to deal with them. For those who have EMD, you are familiar with the "Golden Hour of Trauma." For those that don't, it basically says that if you get trauma help for a critically injured patient within the first hour of trauma, their chances of survival are great. After that hour and each subsequent hour, their chances decrease dramatically. If you are traumatized by a critical incident, start talking about it as soon as possible. Bring that support system together for you. Start that healing process as soon as you can, it can help minimize the affects. You bring those emotions to the surface. And once they are at the surface, it's easier to deal with them rather than having to dig them up.

10. **Have a life outside the job**. Sometimes easier said than done. Law enforcement folks tend to have friends exclusive to law enforcement. That's fine, but having friends outside of law enforcement or firefighting expands our horizons. I've had dispatchers tell me that when they have friends' outside the job, they all want to hear about what we do for a living. Mainly because they don't understand the culture and only understand what they see on TV or in the movies. My advise, for what it's worth, it to tell them up front that you don't want to talk about the rigors of the job while you are off duty. It's your way of taking a break from the stress. If they persist, ask them to talk about their job as a beautician, or forklift operator, or whatever they do for a living. If they respond that their job is not as interesting, invite them down to sit along with you for a shift and perhaps they'll discover for themselves why you don't want to talk about the job. It's worth a try. Variety is the spice of life and it's especially true when it comes to off duty activities and friends. You should not confuse your career with your life.

11. **Understanding of feelings**. If you understand that your feelings may be distressing, they are not by any means dangerous. This goes back to the first step, education about stress. Feelings can't hurt you physically, only actions can.

12. **Change the "what ifs" to "so what's."** As control people, we need to accept that there are some things that can't be controlled. Its not considered apathy, just adjusting your attitude. I've heard dispatchers complain about the way officers sometimes say or phrase things. For example, officers saying "blue in color" or "VIN number." The dispatchers have gotten upset over the terminology. "We know blue is a color." "Why say VIN number when the "N" in VIN stands for number anyway?" So what? As a trained professional, we are expected to be flexible and adaptable. Yes, you know that blue is a color. Yes, you know the "N" in VIN stands for number. Are you going to be able to change what officers say? Is it going to make a difference next year, 5 or 10 years from now? Would it be

any different if they used the phonetic "Whiskey" for the letter "W," rather than the term "William?" You know what they mean. Then why get upset or stressed over it? If you get upset or stressed over something trivial as terminology, then you are setting yourself up for bigger problems down the road. More specific, a heart attack, high blood pressure or hypertension, or a stroke. Let it go. You're the professional, be the professional by not letting the trivial things get to you. Here's a simple way to remember: **"Don't sweat the petty stuff...and while you're at it, don't pet the sweaty stuff"**

13. **Prepare**. I think a simple quote from former UCLA basketball coach John Wooden says it best, "Failure to prepare is preparing to fail." When you were a trainee, did you ever play the "what if" game? What would I do and how would I do it if this were to happen right now? That's called preparing. If you prepare yourself for the eventuality that you will have a critical incident sometime during your career, you are not only preparing for the incident, but the after affects of stress as well. A student of mine once commented about critical incidents and said it very well. She said that a few years back, we used to hope we didn't get one of those officer or firefighter down calls. Now days, it's not a matter of <u>if</u>, but <u>when</u> that call will come in.

14. **Be the best you can be.** That's all anyone can really ask of you. Don't dwell on what went wrong, but with what went right. There are always 10 ways of doing something right, and 10 ways of doing something wrong, and 10,000 ways in between. If your critical incident didn't cause any physical harm to anyone by doing something the wrong, don't spend time dwelling on it. Learn from your mistake and move on. I'll guarantee you probably won't make the same mistake again. That's how we learn. We've been in this learning process since infancy and the process will continue. Its called life. Count your victories.

Surviving and Thriving

Coping at home

As mentioned earlier, we have some of the worst eating habits on earth. We'll eat all the wrong foods for the wrong reasons. And from a personal aspect, it's hard to tell someone that the types of food we eat will affect us years down the road. I know, I was one of those hardheads and now the price is being paid with digestive tract problems. We eat fatty foods, we eat greasy foods, foods high in starch, foods low in nutritional value, and of course, caffeine. The basic food groups for dispatchers would include all of these, including chocolate. But chocolate has at least a value when eaten in moderation. It contains an enzyme that helps make you feel good. I don't recommend eating a five-pound box of chocolate in one sitting, but a little couldn't hurt.

Some of the long term affects of fatty foods are high cholesterol (which can clog arteries), gall bladder problems (including gall stones, something very painful), heart disease, and upper and lower gastrointestinal problems.

A few years ago, UCLA medical center did a study called "7 Rules for Prolonging Life." If you were to practice all of these things regularly, they determined that is was possible to add a certain amount of years to your life. Here's the list, then guess how many years they concluded it could add to your life.

EAT —	Breakfast
EAT —	Three meals a day
Get 7 to 8 —	Hours of sleep
Exercise —	regularly. 20 minutes a day 3 or 4 times a week can be sufficient.
Keep —	Your weight within normal limits.
Drink only — in moderation	
Avoid —	smoking

Pretty simple, huh? Have you formulated an answer? The study said that if you practiced these 7 rules, it would be possible to add 20 years to your life. Of course there are other factors to take into consideration. Family health history, genetics and so forth, but if you are healthy, according to an old Jewish saying, you have everything.

Food. I know we already discussed diets, but this is about a food that helps you relax. What happens after the family dinner at Thanksgiving? It's not so much that we stuff ourselves, it's from the turkey we eat. Warm turkey has an enzyme called tryptophan that helps relax you. You already know what chocolate can do for you, so the next time you feel under pressure or stress and need to relax, try eating a warm turkey sandwich.

Exercise. With the knowledge of some of the long-term affects of eating fatty foods, exercise is an excellent way to help get rid of that fat problem. No, it doesn't mean that you have to join the gym; that would be perfect, but it means that because of our sedentary job, some form of exercise will be greatly beneficial. All it takes is 20 minutes a day 3 or 4 times a week. Just enough to help you break a good sweat. Start off by getting a complete physical from your doctor. Let your doctor know what your intentions are and ask for any recommendations or limitations. Then start off slow. Perhaps taking a walk around the block and gradually working up to a faster pace. Swimming is very good because it works out most of the body's muscles. Even an exercise program that takes place in a pool can provide the aerobic exercise of 20 minutes. Try riding a bicycle and going for a ride 3 or 4 times a week. I suggest you check out the area you will be riding in first. You don't want to make the mistake I made. I bought a mountain bike to start exercising. I got the helmet, the bandanna to wear under the helmet, the biking glasses for both day and night, and biking gloves. I didn't start off slow but jumped right in. Figuring I looked like the consummate bike patrol officer, I decided that I would start riding my bike to work. The first day I left the house feeling really good about my decision. Ten minutes later I was at the station telling myself how wonderful that felt and that it wasn't so hard. At the end of shift, I grabbed my gear and bike and started peddling back home. Much to my surprise, it took me 25 minutes to ride home and was a lot harder going home than coming to work. The reason? Dopey me forgot that it was downhill to work. In my enthusiasm to start riding, I didn't think about the uphill ride at end of watch.

Talking. As repetitive as this sounds, it really is one of the best ways to work those feelings out. Especially with your family and loved ones. Let them know exactly what you have been through and the feelings you have. Express your fears, doubts, concerns or whatever you feel. Your family is your inner circle of support, those closest to you. They know you better than anyone else and they are that safe haven that you can retreat to. Your family will be able to put a different perspective on the situation that maybe you haven't thought of yet. Don't keep them in the dark. If you do, it only makes them feel like you are pushing them away when all they want to do is help. Open up and let them help. Another great way of getting those feelings out is by writing them down. Keep a journal and express yourself. After a period of time, go back and read what you were feeling during that time. You'll surprise yourself at how you have worked through that period.

Relax. Probably one of the hardest things for a type A personality to do is relax. Some of us actually have to learn to relax. Try whatever works best for you, whether it's sitting in a room with your favorite music playing, laying on that hammock in the backyard, reading a good book, sitting by the fire, or watching fish in an aquarium. Try not to have any distractions. Turn off that pager and cell phone for a while, let the answering machine take the call, arrange for the kids to go to the movies or have someone watch them for a while. Be creative in your endeavors, just make the time for yourself. Watch children and puppies at play. If you put the two together and let them go at it, you'll find yourself laughing and wanting to join in. It's one of life's roses that we need to stop and smell along the pathway. "Our ability to relax reflects our willingness to trust." - Anonymous.

Breathing Techniques. Here again, the job we do is sedentary. By sitting most of our shift, our breathing tends to become shallow and we don't utilize our full lung capacity. A technique that trainers instruct their trainees to use to calm down an R/P is to take a deep breath. If someone is hysterical, we tell them to take a deep breath, hold it for a second or two, then release it slowly. If you, as a dispatcher, have been taught this technique and use it to calm people down, try it on yourself. There is a technique called 60 second breathing. It's real simple and you can practice it while sitting at your console. Breathe in slowly and exhale slowly for 10 seconds. Do this 6 times a minute and you have your 60-second breathing technique. If you practice it a couple of times during your shift, it will help you remain calm. Look at it this way; whether you realize it or not, when we are faced with a stressful situation, for the most part, we take a big deep breath as we start to take action. Why not have a little more control over the situation by taking a couple of deep breaths through out the incident. When you are handling a critical incident, sometimes we tend to hunch over the keyboard or writing surface. What that does is take away our full capacity for breathing deeply. It pushes the diaphragm up into the chest cavity so that our lungs don't fully expand. Hence, the need for a couple of deep breaths during the call.

Stretching. Here's another one you can do while sitting at your console. Stretch your neck and rotate your head around. It helps loosen up the muscles in your neck and upper shoulders. Dispatchers tend to hunch their shoulders when working a "hot" call and typing into the CAD. Imagine what that does to your neck and shoulders. If you take your fingers and thumb of one hand and put the tips of them together to form a sort of ball, then balance a bowling ball on top of them, that's what your neck is like trying to hold up your head all the time. Add stress on top of that and it's no wonder we carry around sore neck and shoulder muscles. Stretch your arms up over your head and take a deep breath. Stand up once in a while during your shift and stretch your back and legs. Get the kinks out.

There are even consoles out there that force you to stand. They're programmable and will automatically rise at the prescribed time. They can be programmed to stay at a certain height for a specified time, then they return to their original position. Yes, there is a "kill" switch in case you are working a pursuit at the time. Can you picture the look on a dispatcher's face when in the middle of a pursuit, the console starts to rise? There are also consoles that you can manually raise to achieve the same results.

Cry. All right, here's a tough one. In the business of dispatching, and particularly law enforcement and firefighting, it's frowned upon to show any emotion. Especially for men. Consider what Hal Brown, a licensed clinical social worker who specializes in helping law enforcement deal with the emotions of CIS, says about men showing emotions. "One of the very few benefits to come out of the Vietnam War...is that we learned it's okay for tough guys to cry... and that it's good for them." Society has taught men, and we have been brought up that way, that it's a sign of weakness to cry or show emotion. We're just supposed to "suck it up" and "take it like a man." We bury those feelings deep inside and we don't deal with them. They wind up manifesting themselves later in life with emotional and health problems. It's one reason we die before the women do, guys. If you ask any woman what she feels about a man who cries, she'll probably tell you that it's a sign of strength. After the Gulf War, Connie Chung was interviewing General H. Norman Schwartzkopf on a network news magazine. She asked him about his experiences; a career soldier, two tours of duty in Viet Nam, wounded twice, and now the Supreme Allied Commander of the Gulf War. Then she asked him about his father. There was a long pause and you could see tears welling up in the General's eyes. He didn't speak. Connie Chung commented about the tears when she mentioned his father. The General began to talk about the love he had for his father, how his father taught him everything he knew about life. What we would call the old fashioned love between a father and son. Connie then asked him if he was afraid that his troops would see him cry. He didn't hesitate in his response; "A man who doesn't cry scares me." After the career the General had, the thing that scared him was a man who wouldn't show his emotions. Pretty profound statement. It really is okay for us guys to cry. You know the old saying about a good cry is good for you? Keep this in mind; "Tears unshed make organs weep." What does that say to you? And besides, the beneficial thing about tears is that it's one way the body gets rid of those chemicals that accumulate in our systems during times of stress and grief. Julius Caesar once said, ."..as a rule, men worry about what they can't see than about what they can." Because of our genetic makeup, we want to fix everything and make it better. Why then, won't we take care of ourselves and fix ourselves by letting go with a good cry every now and then?

Toys. All kinds of them. Taking small toys to work with you gives you some distraction during those brief lulls in the action. I know of a center in Northern California where a Communications Supervisor gives out little toys for doing a good job. The dispatchers think of them as their badges of honor. When they come to work, they take all of their toys out of their lockers and set them up at their workstation. At the end of shift, they collect them and put them back in their locker for their next shift. In particular, though, get one of those stress balls. It takes your mind off a stressful event, gives you a form of exercise, and it can make your Risk Management personnel happy because it helps cut down on Carpal Tunnel Syndrome. They come in all shapes, sizes, colors and some are even scented for a form of aroma therapy. You can find them in all kinds of stores and, if you can go to one of your state conferences, vendors are fond of having different shape stress balls with their logos on them. They're more than happy to give them out. It puts their company name out there, but they also will have less items to pack up and take back with them. After one conference, a vendor gave me enough stress balls to take back for every student in a stress class I was teaching the next day.

Time management. Structuring our time is one of the hardest things to accomplish. We tend to put too much to do into too little a time frame. Kind of like stuffing 10 pounds of fertilizer into a 5-pound sack. It's a skill and can be learned. It can also be called setting your priorities. There are classes you can take that teach you how to manage your time and set priorities for what is important to you. If you don't want to spend the money on a class, work out your own system. Get a day planner and write everything you need to do for each day and assign it a priority. Remind you of anything on the job? Assigning priorities? Keep your day planner with you all the time and refer to it often. Don't write down tasks, things to do, appointments and such in any other place but your day planner. After a while, you'll find you have extra time on your hands. Try it. It's like keeping a journal.

Hugs. You want to know why a hug feels so good? It releases a chemical opiate in your brain that makes you feel that way. There is a place in Northern California called the Centre for Living with Dying that helps family and friends cope with death, terminal illnesses and stress. It's where my friend Janet works. They have a room that is filled with every kind of teddy bear imaginable. I finally had the pleasure of visiting that room. It was a powerful feeling looking at all of those teddy bears and thinking about the hugs that have been given to them. And the "hugs" they gave back. I've been told by officers, firefighters and dispatchers sitting in that room hugging a teddy bear is one of the most wonderful experiences. Think about it.

Why are we prone to CIS?

There are several reasons why. You have already completed a couple of exercises in this book that helped you identify some stressors. Perhaps the main reason why we are prone is because we're all Egyptians; we live by denial. We will deny that we are under stress or that something is bothering us. We will hide our emotions, and you now know what burying those emotions can do to us. Why hide those emotions? If we are affected by something, it's because we are human. Emotions are one thing that separate us from animals. When you ask someone how they are doing, what is their usual response? "I'm fine." Below is the acronym for the word fine.

F — frustrated (or you can insert your own "F" word of choice)

I — insecure

N — neurotic

E — emotional

So the next time someone tells you they are fine, you really know how they are feeling.

Here's that control word again. We have that need for control and we sometimes get stressed over things we have no control over. Dispatchers also have a clear sense of right and wrong. When things go wrong, there's another stressor added to the pot. And being that we are action oriented, if there is nothing that we can do in a situation, that's one more stressor added to the recipe.

Misconceptions

There are several misconceptions about stress. Here are just a few; "I always know when I start suffering from stress." "It's all in my head." "Everyone suffers from the same stressors." "Everyone feels the same way I do." "Only weak people suffer from stress." These couldn't be farther from the truth.

You don't always know when you start suffering from stress. It can creep up on you and you don't even know it. It's not only in your head, it's also in your body. Remember that there are physical as well as mental affects of stress. Not everyone has the same triggers. What may set things in motion for one person may not affect another. And by the same token, you may feel signs and symptoms on a stronger level than someone else. That doesn't make you weak in any way, just human.

The Stress Spiral

Most people think that stress is linear. We have a baseline of stress that is the average for us. Throughout the day, our stress levels go up and down, and sometimes go below our average baseline. The baseline is different for every person, but for those of us in Emergency Services, we have a baseline much higher than that of the general population.

It's because we are under more stress and pressure than the general population. If you stop to think about the batting average for a professional baseball player, it is usually around .250 to .300. That means that, on the average, every time they step up to the plate, they get a hit maybe 1 time out of 4 at bats. Think about what kind of money a professional ballplayer gets. Now, what are your wages? And we're expected to be perfect, or "bat a thousand," every time we answer the phone or radio. Does that put more pressure or stress on you than the average ballplayer experiences? Of course it does. We are dealing with lives every time we answer the phone or radio. We have a different set of standards to meet that are well above the professional ballplayer. We are professional telecommunicators!

A good friend and mentor of mine, Janet Childs, gives a great example of how our stress levels go up and down throughout the day. Imagine you are leaving your house to go to work and you find that your car won't start. Your stress level goes up. Your next door neighbor offers to drive you to work so that you won't be late. Your stress level goes down. On the drive to work, you realize that you are getting your evaluation this morning. Your stress level goes up. When you arrive at work, you find out that your supervisor called out sick. Whew, your stress level goes down. Later in the shift, you find out that your spouse or significant other is having an affair and your stress level goes way, way up. You stew and stew and finally come up with the solution to plot the murder of your spouse or significant other...your stress level comes back down. All in humor,

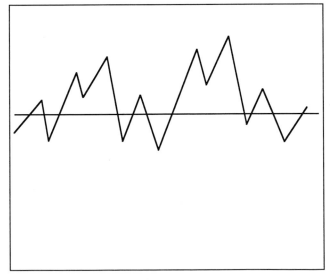

Linear Example of Stress

but that's an example of how our stress levels fluctuate throughout the day. See the example on page 37.

Now for the reality of stress. Stress in not really linear. That's just a simple way showing how our stress levels change during a day. In all actuality, stress is really like a spiral.

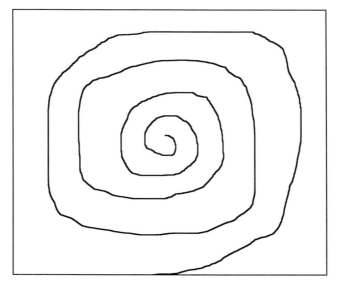

Stress Spiral

All along this spiral, we have what are called landmines or triggers. There can be good landmines and bad landmines. When you hear that favorite song and it takes you back to a happy time, that's a landmine. A landmine, or trigger, can be that call you answered for the child drowning, the structure fire where someone lost their life, or the radio call of an officer down. For me, it's the anniversary date of the officer's down call I described in the beginning of this book. That landmine isn't as strong as it used to be, but I still think about it every week before Christmas.

These land mines or stress triggers have a significant impact on our lives. The effects they have on us later depends on our coping skills and stress relieving techniques. If you handle a critical incident and it has a significant impact on you, think about the next time you handle a similar incident. Will you be able to cope by utilizing some of the techniques and skills you've learned? It does become easier to cope with each incident if you successfully dealt with the stress of the incident. In fact, it will make you stronger and able to cope with stress more effectively. That's not to say that we can't be affected by the emotions of an incident. That's only human, but our coping skills and techniques become sharper.

A year after former Beatle, Paul McCartney lost his wife Linda to breast cancer, he was being interviewed by a member of the media. He was asked if he was able to get over his loss. He responded by saying he hoped he never got over losing his wife, he just wanted to get through it.

Getting through a critical incident never brings that closure. But you can blend it into your life so that it's diluted. You will revisit that incident from time to time. Particularly if you handle a similar call. The previous incident and all its emotions will come back to you. If you have those skills and techniques available to you, you can minimize the affects of stress or grief on your life. Use those tools in your "Dispatcher Toolbox." Instead of building that "wall" of defense, tear down that wall with those tools and you will survive and thrive.

Exercises

The following are some exercises to help you start thinking in terms of how well you cope with stress. There is no scoring. It is designed to help you identify areas of your life that may be affected during stress. If you check a preponderance of the items, it's a sure bet that you are suffering from the affects of stress. If you are concerned about the number of check marks, talk with your doctor or mental health professional for further guidance.

Stress Inventory

Which of the following do you experience at times of stress?
☐ Headaches
☐ Backaches
☐ Muscle spasms
☐ Teeth clenching, awake or during sleep
☐ Trouble getting to sleep
☐ Waking up during the night
☐ Bad dreams
☐ Impotence
☐ Promiscuous sexual activity
☐ Withdrawing from loved ones
☐ Irritability
☐ Becoming argumentative over a variety of things
☐ Excessive aggression on the job
☐ Becoming passive on the job, and/or "hiding"
☐ Poor memory
☐ Poor judgment
☐ Drinking too much or using other drugs
☐ Loss of appetite
☐ Eating too much
☐ Feelings of depression
☐ Mood swings
☐ Angry outbursts

The "stuffing down" or ignorance of distressing emotional reactions is the cause of a lot of problems, not just experiencing these emotional reactions. While our "outer self" is trained and conditioned NOT to be upset by incidents, the "inner self" will experience distress from any of these and other events.

The "outer self" will attempt to cover up these emotions so he/she will appear to be in control, while the "inner self" will feel the distress.

Adapted from Lawrence N. Blum, PhD., Inc.

Writing Exercises

#1 List as many people as you can with whom you have trusted your feelings with in the past.

#2   List people with whom you have not communicated openly with in the past, but have shared their feelings with you

#3 Write down any hobbies or recreational activities you enjoyed as a child or teenager.

#4 List any hobbies or recreational activities that you've often thought of being enjoyable but have never tried.

Humor

As stated before, humor is a great way to deal with stress. In this section you'll find some humorous items, jokes, stories, things you'd like to say to the public but can't and other tidbits. If you find them humorous or they bring a smile to your face, all the better. Many of the authors are unknown, but credit is given where the author is known. If you find one that credit is not given, let us know so credit can be given where credit is due.

A Prayer for the Stressed

Grant me the serenity to accept the things I cannot change,

The courage to change the things I cannot accept,

And the wisdom to hide the bodies of those people I had to kill today because they pissed me off.

And also, help me to be careful of the toes I step on today as. . .

they may be connected to the ass that I may have to kiss tomorrow.

Help me to always give 100 percent at work. . .

12% on Monday

23% on Tuesday

40% on Wednesday

20% on Thursday

and 5% on Friday

And help me to remember that. . .

When I'm having a really bad day,

And it seems that people are trying to piss me off,

That it takes 42 muscles to frown,

And only 4 to extend my middle finger and tell them to bite me.

Author unknown

How to Tell if You're a Dispatcher
(with apologies to Jeff Foxworthy)

You might be a dispatcher if. . .

You answer your home phone "9-1-1 Emergency, where is your emergency?"

The statement "No I don't know him, he's the father of my baby but he don't mean nothing to me" makes perfect sense to you.

Adult police officers, not related to you, refer to you as mother/father.

You consider coffee an indispensable work tool.

You see nothing wrong with eating a Taco Bell Grande Meal or pizza at 3 a.m.

You have the bladder capacity of a small, third world army.

You believe that the statement, "It sure is quiet!" will bring down the wrath of the gods upon you.

You have spent time explaining to a police officer the difference between a dispatcher and a personal assistant.

You live in fear of a full moon.

You are on a first name basis with every crazy lunatic in your jurisdiction.

You find no comfort in knowing that the equipment that you depend on to do your job and protect others was purchased at the lowest bid possible.

You believe that the annual mandatory training classes are purposely scheduled on your day(s) off.

You spend more time discussing clothing color and description than Tommy Hilfiger and Calvin Klein.

You respond faster to the name "Radio" than you do your own name.

You have wanted to meet the guys named "My Babies Daddy" and "Some Dude."

You find yourself talking to your friends and family in codes.

You hear more alien invasion/abduction stories than Scully and Mulder of the X-Files.

You actually believe that you are crushing crime, eradicating evil, saving lives, and snatching people from the jaws of death while singing the theme song to Mighty Mouse: "Mr. Trouble never hangs around. When he hears this mighty sound. 'Here I come to save the day'. That means that Mighty Mouse is on the way."

You get impatient hearing people relate a story when you want "just the facts"

You believe that ninety percent of the population can't look up phone numbers for themselves.

You can easily listen to the TV, radio and screaming kids and not miss a beat.

Your friends and neighbors consult you about their legal matters.

You know the exact address of every bar in your jurisdiction.

You can give directions to anywhere in town off the top of your head.

You have a tendency to giggle at your friends "big" problems.

You can spell out the big words phonetically.

You become easily bored with happy, content people.

You have perfected some witty response to the comment, "I pay your salary!"

Author unknown

Things You'd Love to Say to the Public But Can't...

And your crybaby, whiny-assed opinion would be. . . ?

Do I sound like a people person?

This isn't a Comm Center. . . it's Hell with fluorescent lighting.

I started out with nothing. . .and I still have most of it left.

I pretend to work, they pretend to pay me.

Sarcasm is just one more customer service benefit we offer.

If I throw a stick, will you leave?

You. . .off my planet!

Does your train of thought have a caboose?

Did the aliens forget to remove your anal probe?

And what law school did you graduate from, Matlock?

I'm okay because the voices tell me so.

Am I getting smart with you? No, I'll keep it on your level. (Actually said this to an R/P once. Got in trouble for it, too.)

I'm not your type. I'm not inflatable. (Passed on to me by a friend of mine after she got tired of being hit on by almost every officer in the department)

I'm trying to picture you with a personality.

Stress is when you wake up screaming and you realize you haven't fallen asleep yet.

Sergeant, can I trade this job for what's behind door number 3?

Macho law prohibits me from admitting I made a mistake.

And which one of the Seven Dwarfs are you?

I don't have an attitude problem. You have a perception problem.

I'll bet you put the word "fun" in dysfunctional.

Do you need medical aid because I'll bet you really hurt yourself jumping to that conclusion?

I'd explain it to you, but I'm afraid your brain would explode.

I'm sorry you got a speeding ticket. You feel you don't deserve it? What, did the officer interrupt your qualifying lap?

There are two things on Earth that are universal...hydrogen and stupidity. You don't look like an atomic weapon to me, so that leaves us with one alternative...

Stress Diet

The following diet is designed to help you cope with the stress that builds up during the holidays.

Breakfast:

1/2 grapefruit
1 slice whole wheat toast
8 oz. skim milk

Lunch:

4 oz. lean broiled chicken breast
1 cup steamed spinach
1 cup herb tea
1 Oreo cookie

Mid-Afternoon snack:

The rest of Oreos in the package
2 pints Rocky Road ice cream with nuts, cherries and whipped cream
1 jar hot fudge sauce

Dinner:

2 loaves garlic bread
4 cans or 1 large pitcher of Coke
1 large sausage, mushroom and cheese pizza
3 Snickers bars

Late Evening News:

Entire frozen Sara Lee cheesecake (eat directly from the freezer and out of the box)

RULES FOR THIS DIET:

1. If you eat something and no one sees you eat it, it has no calories.

2. If you drink a diet soda with a candy bar, the calories in the candy bar are canceled out by the diet soda.

3. When you eat with someone else, calories don't count if you do not eat more than they do.

4. Food used for medicinal purposes NEVER count, such as hot chocolate, brandy, toast and Sara Lee cheesecake.

5.   If you fatten up everyone else around you, then you look thinner.

6.   Movie related foods do not have additional calories because they are part of the entertainment package and not part of one's personal fuel. Examples: Milk Duds, buttered popcorn, Junior Mints, Red Hots and Tootsie Rolls.

7.   Cookie pieces contain no calories. The process of breaking them up causes calorie leakage.

8.   Things licked off knives and spoons have no calories if you are in the process of preparing something.

9.   Foods that have the same color have the same number of calories. Examples: spinach and pistachio ice cream; mushrooms and mashed potatoes.

10. Chocolate is a universal color and may be substituted for any other food color

11. Anything consumed while standing has no caloric value. This is due to gravity and the density of the caloric mass.

12. Anything consumed from someone else's plate has no calories since the calories rightfully belong to the other person and will cling to his/her plate. (We all know how calories like to cling)

REMEMBER: STRESSED   SPELLED   BACKWARDS   IS DESSERTS

Author unknown

Chain of Command

Chief of Police: Leaps tall buildings in a single bound; is more powerful than a locomotive; is faster than a speeding bullet; walks on water; gives policy to God.

Captains: Leaps short buildings in a single bound; is more powerful than a switch engine; is as fast as a speeding bullet; walks on water in calm sea; talks with God.

Lieutenants: Leaps short buildings with a running start and favorable winds; is almost as powerful as a switch engine; faster than a speeding BB; walks on water in the backyard wading pool; talks with God when special request is approved.

Sergeants: Barely clears a sleeping bag; loses tug of war with locomotive; can fire a speeding bullet; swims well; is occasionally addressed by God.

Regular Officers: Makes high marks on wall when trying to leap buildings; is often run over by a locomotive; can sometimes handle a gun without inflicting serious self-injury; dog paddles; talks to animals a lot.

Reserve Officers: Runs smack into buildings; can recognize a locomotive two out of three times; is not issued ammunition; cannot stay afloat with a life preserver; talks to walls.

New Recruits: Falls over doorsteps when attempting to enter buildings; says, "Look at the choo-choo!"; shoots themselves with a water pistol; plays in mud puddles; mumbles to themselves.

Dispatchers: Lifts buildings and walks under them; kicks locomotives off the tracks if they are in the way; catches speeding bullets with their teeth and eats them; freezes water with a single glance; they ARE God.

*Author unknown

Little Johnny

Little Johnny's kindergarten class was on a field trip to their local police station where they saw some photographs tacked to a bulletin board. It was the 10 Most Wanted criminals. One of youngsters pointed to a picture and asked if it really was the photo of a wanted person.

"Yes," said the policeman. "The detectives want very badly to capture him."

Little Johnny asked, "Why didn't you keep him when you took his picture?"

Little Johnny's kindergarten class took another field trip to the local police academy. The Tactical Sergeant was standing in front of the class and the class of cadets. He welcomed the students to the academy and then turned to the cadets and said, "Everyone who thinks they are stupid, stand up!"

After a few seconds, Little Johnny stood up. The Tac Sergeant looked at Little Johnny and said, "Son, do you think you're stupid?"

Little Johnny replied, "No sir, but I didn't want you to be standing there all by yourself."

The Tac Sergeant then barked, "Are you trying to make me look like a fool?"

"No sir, you don't need my help," replied Little Johnny.

*Author unknown

Top Ten Reasons Why 9-1-1 is More Than Just a Job:

10. You get a stronger sense of your own humanity by helping others.

9. You get a better feeling about your own loser life compared to the life stories of pathetic RPs

8. Chance to meet, date, marry, & divorce a cop

7. Can do #8 more than once

6. Fashionable uniform prepares you to be a trend-setter – when polyester comes back in

5. Abundance of "challenged" citizens insures job security

4. Tales told by 5150 ["mentally evacuated"] callers are often more entertaining than TV

3. Dealing with the multicultural community allows you to learn swear words in many different languages

2. Potential for being "discovered" when media arrives to cover department screw-ups

1. Can drive like hell and good chance you'll never get a ticket

Author unknown

You Know You're Too Stressed If...

You can achieve a "Runner's High" by sitting up.

The Sun is too loud.

Trees begin to chase you.

You can see individual air molecules vibrating.

You can hear mimes.

You say the same sentence over and over again, not realizing that you have said it before.

You believe that if you think hard enough, you can fly.

Things become "Very Clear,"

You ask the drive-thru attendant if you can get your order to go.

You say the same sentence over and over again, not realizing that you have said it before.

You keep yelling "STOP TOUCHING ME!!!!" even though you are the only one in the room.

Your heart beats in 7/8 time.

You and Reality file for divorce.

You say the same sentence over and over again, not realizing that you have said it before.

You can skip without a rope.

It appears that people are speaking to you in binary code.

You have great revelations concerning: Life, the Universe and Everything else, but can't quite find the words for them before the white glow disappears, leaving you more confused than before.

You say the same sentence over and over again, not realizing that you have said it before.

You can travel without moving.

Antacid tablets, or better known as dispatcher candy, become your sole source of nutrition.

You say the same sentence over and over again, not realizing that you have said it before.

You discover the aesthetic beauty of office supplies.

You have an irresistible urge to bite the noses of the people you are talking to.

Losing your mind was okay, but when the voices in your head quieted, it was like losing your best friend.

Author unknown

Dispatcher Inspiration

We receive inspiration from different things in life. And on many levels. We get inspiration from our loved ones, family, friends, nature, ideas, beliefs and goals to name a few. When we are under stress, a little inspiration goes a long way. It's something we don't think about and, perhaps, need to be reminded of. The following items are some inspirational stories that you might want to read when you are under stress. Here again, many are by unknown authors. Credit is given where the author is known.

Frogs

A group of frogs were traveling through the woods, and two of them fell into a deep pit. All the other frogs gathered around the pit. When they saw how deep the pit was, they told the two frogs that they were as good as dead. The two frogs ignored the comments and tried to jump up out of the pit with all their might. The other frogs kept telling them to stop, that they were as good as dead. Finally, one of the frogs took heed to what the other frogs were saying and gave up. He fell down and died. The other frog continued to jump as hard as he could. Once again, the crowd of frogs yelled at him to stop the pain and just lay down and die. He jumped even harder and finally made it out of the pit. When he got out, the other frogs said, "Did you not hear us?" The frog explained to them with signs that he was deaf. He thought they were encouraging him the entire time.

This story teaches us two lessons:

1. There is power of life and death in the tongue. An encouraging word to someone who is feeling down can lift them up and help them make it through the day.

2. A destructive word to someone who is down can be what it takes to kill them.

Be careful what you say. Speak life to those who cross your path. The power of words. . .it is sometimes hard to understand that an encouraging word can go such a long way. Anyone can speak words that tend to rob another of the spirit to continue in difficult times. Special is the individual who will take the time to encourage another.

*Author unknown

Guardian Angel

Many people will walk in and out of your life, but only true friends will leave footprints in your heart.

To handle yourself, use your head;
To handle others, use your heart.

Anger is only one letter short of danger.

If someone betrays you once, it's their fault;
If they betray you twice, it's your fault.

Great minds discuss ideas;
Average minds discuss events;
Small minds discuss people.

God gives every bird its food,
But He does not throw it into its nest.

He who loses money, loses much;
He who loses a friend, loses more;
He who loses faith, loses all.

Beautiful young people are acts of nature,
But beautiful old people are works of art.

Learn from the mistakes of others.
You can't live long enough to make them all yourself.

The tongue weighs practically nothing,
But so few people can hold it.

Author unknown

Juggling Life

(This is from a University commencement address several years ago. It was given by Brian Dyson, then CEO of Coca-Cola Enterprises on the relation of work to one's other commitments)

"Imagine life as a game in which you are juggling some five balls in the air. You name them "work," "family," "health," "friends," and "spirit" and you're keeping all of these in the air. You will soon understand that work is a rubber ball. If you drop it, it will bounce back. But the other four balls; family, health, friends and spirit are made of glass. If you drop one of these, they will be irrevocably scuffed, marked, nicked, damaged or even shattered. They will never be the same.

You must understand that and strive for balance in your life. How? Don't undermine your worth by comparing yourself with others. It is because we are different that each of us is special. Don't set your goals by what other people deem important. Only you know what is best for you.

Don't take for granted the things closest to your heart. Cling to them as you would your life, for without them, life is meaningless.

Don't let your life slip through your fingers by living in the past or the future. By living your life one day at a time, you live ALL the days of your life.

Don't give up when you still have something to give. Nothing is really over until the moment you stop trying.

Don't be afraid to admit that you are less than perfect. It is this fragile thread that binds us to each other.

Don't be afraid to encounter risks. It is by taking chances that we learn how to be brave.

Don't shut love out of your life by saying it's impossible to find. The quickest way to receive love is to give; the fastest way to lose love is to hold it too tightly; and the best way to keep love is to give it wings.

Don't run through life so fast that you forget not only where you've been, but also where you are going.

Don't forget that a person's greatest emotional need is to feel appreciated.

Don't be afraid to learn. Knowledge is weightless, a treasure you can always carry easily.

Don't use time or words carelessly. Neither can be retrieved.

Life is not a race, but a journey to be savored each step of the way. Yesterday is History, Tomorrow is a Mystery and Today is a gift: that's why we call it – The Present."

Lessons from Geese

By flying in the "V" formation, the whole flock adds 71% greater flying range than if a bird flew alone. As each bird flaps its wings, it creates an "uplift" for the bird that follows.

Lesson: People who share a common direction and sense of community get where they are going quicker and easier because they are traveling on the thrust of one another.

Whenever a goose falls out of formation, it suddenly feels the drag and resistance of flying alone and quickly gets back into the formation to take advantage of the "lifting power" of the bird immediately in the front.

Lesson: If we have as much sense as geese, we will stay in formation with those who are headed where we want to go (and be willing to accept their help as well as give ours to others.)

When the lead goose gets tired, it rotates back into the formation and another goose flies at the point position.

Lesson: It pays to take turns doing the hard or difficult task, and share leadership with people. As with geese, we are mutually dependent on each other.

The geese in the formation honk from behind to encourage those up front to keep up their speed.

Lesson: We need to make sure our honking from behind is encouraging and not something else.

When a goose gets sick or wounded and is forced to drop out of formation, two geese drop out and follow it down and stay with it to help and protect it. They stay with it until it is able to fly again or it dies. Then they launch out on their own until they can join another formation or catch up with their gaggle.

Lesson: If we have as much sense as geese, we too will stand by each other in difficult times, and we will be dedicated to each other's success.

*Author unknown

And God Created Dispatchers

The angel walked in and found the Lord walking around in a small circle muttering to himself.

"What are you working on now Lord?" asked the angel.

"Well, I finished creating a peace officer, now I'm working on a dispatcher."

Since the angel could see nothing in the room, he asked God to tell him about it.

"Its somewhat like the police officer model. It has 5 hands; one for answering the phone, two for typing, one for answering the radio and one for grabbing a cup of coffee. The arms had to be placed fairly carefully since all the tasks a dispatcher does, have to be done simultaneously. The digestive system is a little complicated, since it runs on coffee and food that can be delivered, but seldom needs to get up for the rest room. I made the skin tempered Duralite covered Teflon. A dispatchers hide has to be tough enough to withstand darts from cranky officers, jabs from citizens, and lack of attention by administration, but not show any signs of wear and tear. Unlike a police officer, it only needs one pair of eyes, so that left extra room for the ears. There are five sets ears; one for the telephone, one for the main radio, two for the other radios it has to monitor, and one to hear everything else going on around it. They fit right on the head, since it had to be extra large for the brain. The brain has to be enormous so it can remember a full set of 10 codes, phonetic alphabet, at least two hundred different voices, the entire contents of three different SOP manuals, two teletype manuals, and an NCIC code book. Of course, I left enough extra space for it to learn individual quirks of every different Sergeant, Lieutenant, Watch Commander, fire chief and other supervisors, and the ability to keep them all straight. There also has to be room for it to learn which situations need an officer and which don't, and also the ability to determine in less than two minutes what to do for any given event. There is a built in condenser so it can take an hour long explanation, put it into 30 seconds worth of radio transmission, but still get the whole story across. Those switches in the front are for the emotions. It has to be able to talk to a mother whose child has just died without showing pain, a rape victim and show empathy, a suicidal person and show calmness and reassurance, and an abusive drunk without getting angry. When one of the officers yells for help, it can't panic, and when someone doesn't make it, the dispatcher's heart mustn't break. The little soft spot just to the left of the emotion switch is for abandoned animals, frightened children, and little old ladies who are lonely and just want to talk to someone for a few minutes. The dispatcher has to care very much for the officers and firefighters it serves, without getting personally involved with any of them, so I added another switch for that. Plus, of course, the dispatcher can't have any of its own issues to worry about while it is on duty, so that last switch turns those off. The patience switch is turned up high all the time on the CTO model, and I've added an extra fuse to those to handle the overload. A dispatcher has to be able to function efficiently under less than good physical conditions, and be flexible enough to withstand whatever whim the administration comes up with, while retaining its general shape and form. That warm fuzzy shoulder is there for the officers to use when they gripe, other dispatchers when they hurt, and for those who are shell shocked by a horrible call and just need someone to be there. The voice gave me a little trouble; it has to be clear and easy to understand, calm and even when everyone else is screaming, but still able to convey empathy and caring while remaining totally professional. It runs for a full 12 hours on very little sleep, requires almost no days off, and gets paid less than an executive secretary."

"The dispatcher sounds wonderful Lord," said the angel, "Where is this amazing creation?"

"Well you see," answered the Lord, "dispatchers are invisible unless they make a mistake. So it's practically impossible to tell when they are run down, worn out or in need of repair. Now that I've created them, I can't see the original model to make enough of them to go around."

Author unknown

Dispatcher Prayers

LORD, Thou knowest better than I know myself that I am growing older and will someday be old. Keep me from the fatal habit of thinking I must say something on every subject and on every occasion. Release me from the craving to straighten out everybody's affairs. Make me thoughtful but not moody; helpful but not bossy. With my vast store of wisdom, it seems a pity not to use it all, but thou knowest, Lord, that I want a few friends at the end.

Keep my mind free from the recital of endless details; give me the wings to get to the point. Seal my lips on my aches and pains. They are increasing and love of rehearsing them is becoming sweeter as the years go by. I dare not ask for grace enough to enjoy the tales of others pains, but help me to endure them with patience.

I dare not ask for improved memory, but for a growing humility and a lessing cocksureness when my memory seems to clash with the memories of others. Teach me the glorious lesson that occasionally I may be mistaken.

Keep me reasonably sweet; I do not want to be a Saint; some of them are so hard to live with. But a sour old person is one of the crowning works of the devil. Give me the ability to see good things in unexpected places, and talents in unexpected people. And give me, O Lord, the grace to tell them so.

AMEN

Author unknown

Dispatcher Prayer

Lord, they're in our hands tonight, Yours and mine.
Those "folks" who keep the peace and fight the crime.
They're men with wives, "women with husbands" and families,
and feelings too.
They give themselves for our protection, these "folks" in blue.

I know my part in this is crucial too.
I must inform those "folks" in blue.
When trouble strikes, and where.
And send them quickly, no time to spare.

I cannot see the scene from where I sit.
My eyes and ears scan the console, brightly lit.
I must wait in blind suspense to hear each "ten-four,"
As they let me know they have survived one time more.

I know a part of them that few others see-
Their eyes reflecting scenes depicting how cruel life can really be.
A battered child, a senseless wreck, or a murderer set free,
A brother-in-arms shot down, never more be.

I'll make coffee, and keep it fresh and strong,
They'll stop by for a cup or two, but not for long.
Another call, a plea, or just a happenstance.
Duty will beckon, "Come, time to take another chance."

I'll answer the phone and questions, too.
And dig out the stats and records they ask me to.
I'll type the reports, and of course, joke with them some.
I'll even put off that reporter who calls in on "nine-one-one."

Let me, Lord, speak calm and clear,
To these out there while I'm in here.
I'm their link, and they are mine.
In this partnership of fighting crime.

It seems to me that we're all a team.
They, You, and me, I mean.
I'll do my best, and they will too.
But, still, Lord, we need You to see us through.

AMEN

Author unknown

Dispatcher Prayer

As I sit here it is all to quiet.
I'm thankful to have such a peaceful night.
To catch up on paperwork, or read a good book.
The town is asleep it seems, even the crooks.
Although they are in service, and my officers have not called,
I check on them anyway, making sure it's safe with them.

Later in the morning hours, I hear a static squelch,
The only audible voice I hear says, "Base I need some help!"
I recognize his voice, but I don't know his location.
Quickly I send all other cars to his assigned patrol.
"Search all areas," I call to them, "until he says it's under control."

The situation is ultimately tense.
I must remain calm-I must keep my sense.
As my palms become sweaty, my heart begins to pound.
I pray, "God, don't let them find him on the ground!"
The seconds pass like hours. "Where are YOU!!"
I scream in my head. I call for his location and again, nothing is
said.

I know the officers that are en route,
are responding as fast as they can.
"Step it up," I snap on the radio waves.
"We've got to find this man."

An officer reports that he is on the scene,
"I'll be out of the car!"
But in his moment of desperation, he doesn't tell me where they
are.

Finally, a second backup arrives.
The location he is able to provide.
"All other cars start that way until SOMEBODY tells me that it
is OK!"

My heart begins to rest a bit,
but not enough to feel good.
Not until every officer I have is in that neighborhood.

Many more officers are with him now,
they tell me that they are not hurt.
"We have one in custody. We're en route to the jail with this jerk!"
He is booked and processed, pictured and printed.
He sits all alone as if serving a life sentence.

The officers are through at the jail now.
They are going back to their beats.
But they hesitate as they pass my office. Taking time to speak.
"You ought to come and work with us, out here in this war.
You'll never know excitement here, sitting behind these doors."

I let them think what they want to think and say what they want
to say.
Little do they know the excitement I have,
taking care of them each and every day!

Who Am I

I am the voice that calms the mother
breathing life into her infant son.
I am the invisible hand that holds and comforts the elderly man,
who woke up and found his wife of 50 years had passed away
during the night.

I am the friend who talks the disgruntled teenager
out of ending her life.
I sent help when you had your first automobile accident

I am the one who tries to obtain the information
from callers to ensure that the scene is safe
for those I dispatch to emergencies,
all the while anticipating the worst and hoping for the best.

I am the psychologist who readily adapts
by language and tone of voice to serve the needs
of my callers with compassion and understanding.
I am the ears that listen to the needs of all those I serve.

I have heard the screams of faceless people
I will never meet or forget.
I have cried at the atrocities of mankind
and rejoiced at the miracles of life.

I was there, though unseen by my comrades
in the field during the most trying emergencies.
I have tried to visualize the scene to coincide with the voices I
have heard.

I am usually not privy to the outcome of a call, and so I wonder...

I am the one who works weekends, strange shifts and holidays.
Children do not say they want my job when they grow up.
Yet, I am at this vocation by choice.
Those I help do not call back to say thank you.
Still, there is comfort in the challenge, integrity and the purpose
of my employment.

I am thankful to provide such a meaningful service.
I am mother, a father, sister, brother, son or a daughter.
I am here when you need me and still here when you don't.
My office is never empty, and the work is never done.

I am always on call.
The training is strenuous, demanding and endless.
No two days at work are ever the same.

Who am I?
I am an emergency dispatcher and I am proud.

By Tracy Cameron
Orlando, FL Fire Department

Letter to a Veteran Police Officer

Have you ever wondered what dispatchers think of you?
It's hard for us to understand the hell that you go through.
You told me once that you have been a cop for many years.
You briefly talked of good times, but never your fears.

Everyday you prattle on, your chatter fills the air.
I sometimes wonder if you have a clue who's in my chair.
My nerves seem wrapped around my throat; I wait for your "10-4."
I breathe a little better when I hear your voice once more.

Life would become difficult for those you left behind,
If you were cut down needlessly by a fool who lost his mind.
I imagine that it's on your mind each time you draw your gun.
I think about it every day before my work is begun.

I see the black band on your badge and it gives me a chill.
To recognize the darkest evil lives in this world still.
I force myself to smile when I know you're watching me.
I'm hoping that you'll never ask, "Is that a tear I see?"

It troubles me to think that I may not hear you again.
You're much more than a cop to me - you have been a friend.
If anything should happen, I would miss you every day.
I promise you I'll do my best so harm won't come your way.

But sometimes I don't have control; it's then I say a prayer.
Help me, Lord, to keep them safe - let them know I care.
Don't let them know I worry, just let them be all right.
I pray that You'll be with them throughout the day and night.

Lord, if their lives are ended by a bullet, crash or knife,
I ask that You would be there with their grieving husband or wife.
Let their children be comforted, knowing until the end
It was the good of all mankind their parent did defend.

There's never time to say this when I'm on the radio,
But I have two things to ask of you, old cop, before I go.
I really do respect you; you've survived the job this long.
Please answer when I call you, and forgive me when I'm wrong.

By Michele M. Hriciso

A Tribute to Dispatchers

Someone once asked me if I thought that answering telephones for a living was a profession. I said, "I thought it was a calling."

And so is dispatching. I have found in my law enforcement career that dispatchers are the unsung heroes of public safety. They miss the excitement of riding in a speeding car with lights flashing and sirens wailing. They can only hear of the bright orange flames leaping from the burning building. They do not get to see the joy on the face of worried parents as they see their child begin breathing on its own, after it has been given CPR.

Dispatchers sit in darkened rooms looking at computer screens and talking to voices from faces they never see. It's like reading a lot of books, but only half of each one.

Dispatchers connect the anxious conversations of terrified victims, angry informants, suicidal citizens and grouchy officers. They are the calming influence of all of them - the quiet, competent voices in the night that provide the pillars for the bridges of sanity and safety. They are expected to gather information from highly agitated people who can't remember where they live, what their name is, or what they just saw. And then, they are to calmly provide all that information to the officers, firefighters, or paramedics without error the first time and every time.

Dispatchers are expected to be able to do five things at once - and do them well. While questioning a frantic caller, they must type the information into a computer, tip off another dispatcher, put another caller on hold, and listen to an officer run a plate for a parking problem. To miss the plate numbers is to raise the officer's ire; to miss the caller's information may be to endanger the same officer's life. But, the officer will never understand that.

Dispatchers have two constant companions, other dispatchers and stress. They depend on one, and try to ignore the other. They are chastened by upset callers, taken for granted by the public, and criticized by the officers. The rewards they get are inexpensive and infrequent, except for the satisfaction they feel at the end of a shift, having done what they were expected to do.

Dispatchers come in all shapes and sizes, all races, both sexes, and all ages. They are blondes, and brunettes, and redheads. They are quiet and outgoing, single, or married, plain, beautiful, or handsome. No two are alike, yet they are all the same. They are people who were selected in a difficult hiring process to do an impossible job. They are as different as snowflakes, but they have one thing in common. They care about people and they enjoy being the lifeline of society – that steady voice in a storm – the one who knows how to handle every emergency and does it with style and grace; and, uncompromised competence.

Dispatchers play many roles; therapist, doctor, lawyer, teacher, weatherman, guidance counselor, psychologist, priest, secretary, supervisor, politician, and reporter. And few people must jump through the emotional hoops on the trip through the joy of one callers birthday party, to the fear of another callers burglary in progress, to the anger of a neighbor blocked in their drive, and back to the birthday callers all in two minutes time frame. The emotional roller coaster rolls to a stop after an 8 or 10 hour shift, and they are expected to walk down to their car with steady feet and no queasiness in their stomach - because they are dispatchers. If they hold it in, they are too closed. If they talk about it, they are a whiner. If it bothers them, it adds more stress. If it doesn't, they question themselves, wondering why.

Dispatchers are expected to have:
—the compassion of Mother Theresa;
—the wisdom of Solomon;
—the interviewing skills of Oprah Winfrey;
—the gentleness of Florence Nightingale;
—the patience of Job;
—the voice of Barbara Streisand;
—the knowledge of Einstein;
—the answers of Ann Landers;
—the humor of David Letterman;
—the investigative skills of Sgt. Joe Friday;
—the looks of Melanie Griffin or Don Johnson;
—the faith of Billy Graham;
—the energy of Charo;
—and the endurance of the Energizer Bunny.

Is it any wonder that many drop out during training? It is a unique and talented person who can do this job and do it well. And, it is fitting and proper that we take a few minutes or hours this week to honor you for a job that each of you do. That recognition is overdue and it is insufficient. I have tried to do your job, and I have failed. It takes a special person with unique skills. I admire you and I thank you for the thankless job you do. You are heroes, and I am proud to work with you.

Chief of Police Tom Wagoner
Loveland, Colorado PD
April 12, 1994

Officer Inspirational

One of the worst nightmares a dispatcher can face is the loss of an officer or firefighter in the line of duty. The second worse thing we can face, is the loss of an officer or firefighter off duty. Losing a co-worker either way, is one of the most horrible and frustrating experiences you may have to endure. The following are a tribute to those who have made the ultimate sacrifice, either on or off duty. Others are for those who are still on the beat or waiting to answer the call for help.

Tears of a Cop

I have been where you fear to go...
I have seen what you fear to see...
I have done what you fear to do...
All of these things I've done for you.

I am the one you lean upon...
The one you cast your scorn upon...
The one you bring your troubles to...
All these people I've been for you.

The one you ask to stand apart...
The one you feel should have no heart...
The one you call the man in blue...
But I am human just like you.

And through the years I've come to see...
That I'm not what you ask of me...
So take this badge and take this gun...
Will you take it? Will anyone?

And when you watch a person die...
And hear the battered baby cry...
Then so you think that you can be...
All of those things you ask of me.

Author unknown

Lousy Cop

Dear Mr./Mrs. Citizen

Well, I guess you have me figured out. I seem to fit neatly into the category you place me in. I'm stereotyped, characterized, standardized, classified, grouped, and always typical. I am the lousy cop.

Unfortunately, the reverse isn't true. I can never figure you out. From birth you teach your children that I am a person to beware of. Then, you are shocked when they identify me with my traditional enemy, the criminal. You accuse me of coddling juveniles, until I catch your kid doing something wrong.

You take an hour for lunch, and several coffee breaks each day, then point me out as a loafer if you see me have just one cup of coffee.

You pride yourself on your polished manners, but think of nothing of interrupting my meals at noon with your troubles. You raise hell about the guy who cuts you off in traffic, but let me catch you doing the same thing, and all of a sudden I am picking on you. You know ALL the traffic laws, but never got one single ticket you deserved.

You shout "Abuse of Authority" if you see me driving fast to an emergency call, but raise 9 kinds of hell if I take more than 30 seconds responding to yours. You call it "part of my job" if someone hits me, but yell "Police brutality" if I strike back. You would never think of telling your dentist how to pull a badly decayed tooth, or your doctor how to take out your appendix, but, you are ALWAYS willing to give me pointers on how to be a police officer.

You talk to me in a manner, and use language that would assure a bloody nose from anyone else, but, you expect me to stand there and take your verbal abuse without batting an eye. You cry, "Something has to be done about crime," but you can't be bothered to get involved. You have no use for me what so ever, but of course, it's OK for me to change a tire for your wife, or deliver your baby in the back seat of my patrol car en route to the hospital, or save your son's life with CPR and mouth to mouth resuscitation, or even forsake time with MY family working long hours overtime trying to find your lost daughter.

So, dear citizen, you stand there on your soapbox and rant and rave about the way I do my job, calling me every name in the book, but, never stop a minute to think your property, your family, and maybe your life might someday depend on one thing...me.

Respectfully,

A Lousy Cop

Police Officer Prayer

Lord, God, let me never forget that the police officer stands watch between the powers of hell and your people.

Strengthen my sense of courage, duty and humor during this hour,

keep me safe in body and spirit, and bring me home safely.

Amen.

*Author unknown

For more police officer prayers, check out the following web site address:

SOVER.NET/~TMARTIN/POEMS.HTM

*Most prayers, poems and inspirational writings regarding police officers are copyrighted material. The web site has a very comprehensive listing of those materials.

Firefighter Inspirational

Firefighters have always been considered America's heroes. They are called upon to perform acts of bravery every day. They are called upon when there is no one else to call. The ultimate sacrifice of losing a firefighter in the line of duty is no less devastating than losing a member of law enforcement.

A Firefighter's Prayer

When I am called to duty, God, wherever flames may rage,
give me strength to save some life, whatever their age.

Help me embrace a little child before it is too late,
to save an older person from the horror of that fate.

Enable me to be alert and hear the weakest shout,
and quickly and efficiently to put the fire out.

I want to fill my calling and give the best in me,
to guard my every neighbor and protect their property.

And if I am to lose my life according to my fate, please bless with your protecting hand, my children and my mate.

*Author unknown

A True Hero

"If Prometheus was worthy of the wrath of heaven for kindling the first fire upon earth, how ought the gods to honor the men who make it their professional business to put it out?"

John Godfrey Saxe
American journalist, poet and lecturer
circa 1850

"Firefighters are the only ones to run into burning buildings when everyone else is running out"

*Author unknown

"Fireman are going to be killed right along. They know it, every man of them...firefighting is a hazardous occupation; it is dangerous on the face of it, tackling a burning building. The risks are plain...Consequently, when a man becomes a fireman, his act of bravery has already been accomplished."

Chief Edward F. Croker
New York Fire Department
1908

What is a Fireman?

He's the guy next door, a man's man with the memory of a little boy.
He has never gotten over the excitement of engines and sirens and danger.
He's a guy like you and me with warts and worries and unfulfilled dreams.
Yet he stands taller than most of us.
He's a fireman.

He puts it all on the line when the bell rings.
A fireman is at once the most fortunate and the least fortunate of men.
He's a man who saves lives because he has seen too much death.
He's a gentle man because he has seen the awesome power of violence out of control.

He's responsive to a child's laughter because his arms have held too many small bodies that will never laugh again.
He's a man who appreciates the simple pleasures of life, hot coffee held in thumb and unbending fingers, a warm bed for bone and muscle compelled beyond feeling, the camaraderie of brave men.

He doesn't wear buttons or wave flags our shout obscenities.
When he marches, it is to honor a fallen comrade.
He doesn't preach the brotherhood of man.
He lives it.

Author unknown

Admiration!

This poem was written by Firefighter Carleen Cochran in admiration of her father, Fire Chief Tom Stevens.

Next to the big fire truck I stood.
My throat was scratchy, my legs felt like wood.

I knew in my heart someday I'd sit up in that cab.
Right up there with the firefighters and my dad.

Yup, I'm a firefighters kid, I am, I am.
And someday they'll call me firefighter 'mam!

I'm going to grow up and be just like my dad.
Grow up and ride in that big yellow cab.

I'll get up in the middle of the night, just like dad, to the tone.
Rush out the door, let out a load groan.

Then rush back to the room to put on clothes I forgot.
And out to the truck, my heart racing, my stomach in a knot.

Then I'd stop and look up to the house and wave,
To my kid standing in the doorway telling me to be brave.

You Never Know

The Teacher

There is a story many years ago of an elementary teacher. Her name was Mrs. Thompson. And she stood in front of her 5th grade class on the very first day of school, she told the children a lie. Like most teachers, she looked at her students and said that she loved them all the same. But that was impossible, because there in the front row, slumped in his seat, was a little boy named Teddy.

Mrs. Thompson had watched Teddy the year before and noticed that he didn't play well with the other children, that his clothes were messy and that he constantly needed a bath. And Teddy could be unpleasant.

It got to the point where Mrs. Thompson would actually take delight in marking his papers with a broad red pen, making bold X's and putting a big "F" at the top of his papers. At the school where Mrs. Thompson taught, she was required to review each child's past records and she put Teddy's off until last. However, when she reviewed his file, she was in for a surprise. Teddy's first grade teacher wrote, "Teddy is a bright child with a ready laugh. He does his work neatly and has good manners. . .he is a joy to have around."

His second grade teacher wrote, "Teddy is an excellent student, well liked by his classmates, but he is troubled because his mother has a terminal illness and life at home must be a struggle."

His third grade teacher wrote, "His mother's death has been hard on him. He tries to do his best but his father doesn't show much interest and his home life will soon affect him if some steps aren't taken."

Teddy's fourth grade teacher wrote, "Teddy is withdrawn and doesn't show much interest in school. He doesn't have many friends and sometimes sleeps in class." By now Mrs. Thompson realized the problem and she was ashamed of herself. She felt even more worse when her students brought her Christmas presents, wrapped in beautiful ribbons and bright paper, except for Teddy's. His present, which was clumsily wrapped in the heavy, brown paper bag that he got from a grocery bag. Mrs. Thompson took pains to open it in the middle of the other presents.

Some of the children started to laugh when she found a rhinestone bracelet with some of the stones missing, and a bottle that was one quarter full of perfume. She stifled the children's laughter when she exclaimed how pretty the bracelet was, putting it on, and dabbing some of the perfume on her wrist. Teddy stayed after school that day just long enough to say, "Mrs. Thompson, today you smelled just like my mom use to."

After the children left, she cried for at least an hour. On that very day, she quit teaching reading, and writing and arithmetic. Instead, she began to teach children.

Mrs. Thompson paid particular attention to Teddy. As she worked with him, his mind seemed to come alive. The more she encouraged him, the faster he responded. By the end of the year, Teddy had become one of the smartest children in the class and, despite her lie that she would love all the children the same, Teddy became one of her "teacher's pets."

A year later, she found a note under her door, from Teddy, telling her that she was still the best teacher he ever had in his whole life. Six years went by before she got another note from Teddy. He then wrote that he had finished high school, third in his class, and she was still the best teacher he had in his whole life.

Four years after that, she got another note letter, saying that while things had been tough at times, he'd stayed in school, had stuck with it, and would soon graduate from college with the highest of honors. He assured Mrs. Thompson that she was still the best and favorite teacher he ever had in his whole life.

Then four more years passed and yet another letter came. This time he explained that after he got his bachelor's degree, he decided to go a little further. The letter explained that she was still the best and favorite teacher he ever had. But now his name was a little longer, the letter was signed Theodore F. Stoddard, M.D.

The story doesn't end there. You see, there was yet another letter that spring. Teddy said he'd met this girl and was going to be married. He explained that his father had died a couple of years ago and he was wondering if Mrs. Thompson might agree to sit in the place at the wedding that was usually reserved for the mother of the groom.

Of course, Mrs. Thompson did. And guess what? She wore that bracelet, the one with several rhinestones missing. And she made sure she was wearing the perfume that Teddy remembered his mother wearing on their last Christmas together.

They hugged each other, and Dr. Stoddard whispered in Mrs. Thompson's ear, "Thank you Mrs. Thompson for believing in me. Thank you so much for making me feel important and showing me that I could make a difference." Mrs. Thompson, with tears in her eyes, whispered back. She said, "Teddy, you have it all wrong. You were the one who taught me that I could make a difference. I didn't know how to teach until I met you."

Author unknown

Friendship

His name was Fleming, and he was a poor Scottish farmer. One day, while trying to make a living for his family, he heard a cry for help coming from a nearby bog. He dropped his tools and ran to the bog. There, mired to his waist in black muck, was a terrified boy, screaming and struggling to free himself.

Farmer Fleming saved the lad from what could have been a slow and terrifying death. The next day, a fancy carriage pulled up to the Scotsman's sparse surroundings. An elegantly dressed nobleman stepped out and introduced himself as the father of the boy Farmer Fleming had saved.

"I want to repay you," said the nobleman. "You saved my son's life.

"No, I can't accept payment for what I did, " the Scottish farmer replied, waving off the offer. At that moment, the farmer's own son came to the door of the family hovel. "Is that your son?" the nobleman asked.

"Yes, " the farmer replied proudly.

"I'll make you a deal. Let me take him and give him a good education. If the lad is anything like his father, he'll grow to a man you can be proud of.."

And that he did. In time, Farmer Fleming's son graduated from St. Mary's Hospital Medical School in London, and went on to become known throughout the world as the noted Sir Alexander Fleming, the discoverer of Penicillin.

Years afterward, the nobleman's son was stricken with pneumonia. What saved him? Penicillin. The name of the nobleman? Lord Randolph Churchill. His son's name? Sir Winston Churchill.

Author unknown

Heart Hotel

I've mentioned Janet Childs several times in this book. One of the most touching things she teaches to dispatchers is the "Heart Hotel."

Many years ago, she was talking with a homeless woman who was suffering from an incurable disease. During one of their conversations, Janet mentioned to the woman that she felt she had a wonderful outlook on life and death. She asked the woman how she maintained such a great outlook in view of the fact that she was suffering a debilitating disease. The woman explained it as this:

You have many people come and go in your life. Some may walk in and stay for a short time, while others may stay longer. And then, of course, you have those who stay for a life time. As we get older, we lose some of those close to us. Whether they leave of their own accord, or death takes them, they leave some kind of memento, impression or mark on our lives. If you think of your heart as a hotel, everyone who has been close to us has a room in that hotel. If that person goes away, you still have that room in your heart that you can go and visit the memories of that person. Inside that room, you can spend time dusting off those memories, sitting on the couch and reminiscing, and perhaps, rearranging those memories. You can bring back those times that mean so much to us, those things that we hold dear about that person. No one can ever take that room away or move into that room. Some may have a room, others may have a suite, and others may have a whole floor. You can even build onto your hotel. You can visit those rooms anytime you choose and visit those memories, just don't ever turn the "Vacancy" sign off.

Stories of Survival

There are as many stories of surviving critical incident stress in dispatchers as there are stars in the heavens. The following stories are true. They are stories of incidents where the dispatcher suffered some aspect of critical incident stress. My gratitude goes out to these dispatchers who offered to share their stories. It is not an easy thing to put yourself up for scrutiny and show our vulnerable side. The hope with these dispatchers was to show you that even though their incident may have been the most horrific event they ever handled, they survived.

As you read the stories, think of what you have already learned and see if you can pick out any signs or symptoms, land mines or triggers, and any coping skills and techniques that were utilized to survive.

The names in the stories have been changed. It was our feeling to protect those who may still be feeling vulnerable. Although confidentiality has NOT been compromised, the feelings are too personal to offer up personal names.

Karen from Iowa

Karen had been a dispatcher for 10 years at the time of her critical incident. It was Easter Sunday. Just another slow Sunday for many dispatchers. Domestic disputes and violence are always in the back of a dispatcher's mind on holidays. Out of all of the days of the year, holidays are known for family arguments and fights.

9-1-1 rang. The call was answered and a child of 10 began saying his dad had a gun and was going to kill his mother. Now, with most comm centers, 9-1-1 prank calls become more prevalent, as had been happening prior to this particular 9-1-1 call. As Karen began questioning the caller, he stated that he couldn't talk anymore or his dad would get mad. He said he had to go, then the line went dead.

Karen's first thought was, "Is this for real?," keeping in mind the numerous prank calls that had been received prior to the holiday. As with any dispatcher, officer safety being of paramount concern, and not knowing if the call was a prank, she dispatched the call as the "real" thing. As Karen was putting the call out, her partner received another 9-1-1 call from the neighbor of the first call. They were reporting shots fired. The nightmare began.

There was little radio traffic or cell phone calls from officers at the scene. What Karen and her partner did hear over the radio after a while, was that the scene was secure. They both waited for what seemed like an eternity for some information about what had happened. Then the O-I-C (Officer-in-Charge) called dispatch on his cell phone, "What we have here is a multiple homicide and suicide. Dispatch the SRT (SWAT)," he requested. The dispatchers thought the callout was to assist in securing the crime scene and to keep the media and on-lookers out of the scene. They assumed that it was done and over with and, according to protocol, started calling and paging the homicide team. The first one on the list was a detective named Tom. He was appraised of the situation and advised to respond to the scene.

After the on duty shift was relieved, they were told that there would be a debriefing and that they were requested to attend. During the debriefing, the group was told that they learned a lot from this particular situation, as one of their own detectives was almost shot. Karen was in shock and horrified that the first detective she called, Tom, was almost shot. The dispatchers had not been advised that one of "their" detectives was almost shot during the incident. Karen immediately felt guilt set in. She felt that maybe she hadn't communicated some aspect of vital information to Tom, and that may have contributed to his almost being shot. She had gone home after the debriefing and composed a letter to the Dispatch Supervisor accepting full responsibility for the near tragedy.

The following day at work, Karen discovered that her letter had gone up the Chain of Command to the Chief. She was surprised at the support she received from Administration. She was called aside, one-by-one, and explained to her that what had almost happened to Tom was not her fault. It was then she learned what had happened.

Tom, the detective, had responded to the scene in his private vehicle. At the perimeter, barricades had been set up. He ran the barricade by jumping his vehicle up over the curb. The officers on the perimeter, thinking that it was another member of the family there to seek revenge on the shooter, did not recognize the detective, and drew their weapons on him. The thing that saved him was the baseball hat he was wearing that simply said, "Police."

Knowing that it wasn't her fault, the guilt did not go away. Her peers supported her, the officers supported her, and Administration supported her. The tapes of the call were played and there was no fault to be found. One Captain, who was in dispatch during the incident, told her that he observed that she did a great job.

Still, she felt that she did something wrong. She thought that everything that her co-workers were telling her, were things that she wanted to hear and not really what they meant. Until she attended a critical incident stress management class. It came to her that what everyone was doing was giving her support. She didn't recognize it as being support. It finally made sense to her after she attended the class.

Sadly, part of the 9-1-1 tape was released to the media, and she received some flak from dispatchers from another agency about the way she handled the call. What helped her cope with the criticism was a comment her Captain had made, and was reinforced by her CISM class instructor. She was told not to worry about what others may say, they weren't in the hot seat during the incident. It finally made sense to her.

Shortly after the Easter Sunday incident, Karen and her partner had to deploy their SRT on another call. Karen said, "I actually got a sick feeling in my stomach. I thought, I'm not handling Easter Sunday, even now. Now I understand why it was a stressor for me hearing the term, SRT."

That was the end of the story. The beginning of her story actually started several years earlier, before she became a dispatcher.

She had returned home with her daughter after an afternoon at the movies. When she entered the house, her husband was sitting in the living room fondling his revolver. She asked him what he was doing and he told her he was cleaning it. She questioned him as to where the cleaning supplies were. He told her that he had just started and hadn't gotten them out, yet. He then sat there a while longer, and then put the gun away saying he'd clean it later. She blew off the incident without a second thought.

Until several weeks later when there was a similar incident. This time, she called the police. They surrounded the house and her husband surrendered. He was admitted for psychiatric evaluation. The attending psychiatrist claimed he saw no symptoms of suicidal tendencies and so, her husband was released. On Memorial Day weekend the same year, her husband committed suicide by driving his vehicle off of a road.

In this profession, just when you think you've handled it all, Mr. Murphy invites himself back into the dispatch center. Recently, Karen was confronted with a similar Easter Sunday call. A thirteen year old female called on 9-1-1. She was petrified, her voice filled with terror. She told Karen that her dad had beaten her.

Karen immediately went into gear. She asked lots of questions; there would be no misunderstandings of information. Then the female spoke the words that dispatchers dread during a domestic dispute, "He's going to get his gun!"

Karen's partner was out of the room on a break. No time to hesitate. For a brief moment, her first thought was, "Oh God, not again!" She immediately told the caller to get out of the house and run to a neighbor's house and stay there until officers arrived. "Okay, I gotta go.," replied the caller. It was the same words the little boy had spoken on Easter Sunday.

The call was dispatched. The officers were advised of the gun. The incident went like a well oiled clock. No problems, no shots fired, one in custody. The suspect had 6 guns confiscated that were loaded and waiting. A family disaster adverted.

When it was all over, Karen began to shake. Her first thought was, "Is this some kind of a joke?" She received two similar calls of a father enraged with his family, had possession of weapons, and a child calling 9-1-1. The more she thought about the similarities, the more she shook.

Then her CISM training kicked in. She needed some sort of diversion, something to help release the built up adrenaline. What did she do? Can't leave the center to exercise, jog or do some other form of physical activity. She played a game on her computer terminal. Nothing too strenuous, but it was immediate and it took her mind off of the call. As she played the game, she noticed that she was starting to calm down. The next thing she realized was that there wasn't any guilt like there was on the Easter Sunday incident. She realized that she had more control over this call, even though she had no control over what was happening on the other end of the 9-1-1 call. Her coping skills were becoming sharper, albeit, the technique used was somewhat unorthodox, but she did something. She took care of herself.

Warriors and White Roses

*(**Warning**: This story contains some language that may be offensive to some readers. It is the personal story of a dispatcher that relates words that were either spoken or thought of.)*

This story begins in the morning of the first week of a new year; that didn't seem new at all. I was on my way home from an overtime shift where I worked as a emergency dispatcher for a large, busy, and always understaffed dispatch center for a Southern California sheriff's department.

Body fatigue had set in as I listened to and sang along with country music on the radio while mentally reviewing a conversation that I had with a co-worker during the shift. My car was on semi-auto pilot. (Semi-auto pilot is a feature not listed on the nearly impossible to remove price sticker on the window of the vehicle prior to purchase. Salesmen don't talk about it, but you know you have it when you are driving down a familiar road and you suddenly realize your exit is next and your last cognitive traveling point was five miles and 2 seconds ago.) Feeling lucky that my car knew the way home, I turned down the radio, stopped singing and looked around to make sure I had not had an audience. I was looking forward to my ritual of stopping at the local convenience store to grab a cup of coffee and conduct a mutually agreed upon language lesson with the clerk. Making the turn into the store's driveway, I saw two male "gang bangers" standing in front of the door. Momentarily I considered aborting my planned stop as thoughts of being car jacked crossed my mind, but long established caffeine addiction quieted my fears. I parked and walked between the two young men (making note of their descriptions) and greeted them with a good morning. The one on my left said, "Nice car." I thought, "OOPS," and entered the store.

Having purchased my coffee and extended the language lesson, hoping to no avail that the two gentlemen would leave, I began to walk the gauntlet to my car with keys laced in between my fingers of one hand and hot coffee in the other. Exiting the store, I noticed that the subject on my right had a white item in his hand that he was twisting. *"Not a weapon, good enough."* I continued on to my vehicle. Just as I reached the vehicle's door, the guy that had been twisting the white object hollered, "Wait a minute." My body went hot as I turned expecting the worst and hoping the clerk inside would display his newly acquired pronunciation of the word "robbed" to the 9-1-1 dispatcher should this moment go the way of my fears. Turning toward the voice, my eyes went directly to his hands and was able to identify the white object. It was paper! He quickly finished the last few twists on the paper and in one movement flipped what was now a white object over and extend it in an almost child like movement toward me. It was a white paper rose. I palmed my keys and stepped forward accepting his gift and asking him where he had learned to make a white rose. He went into detail about his past when he was "banging" and got shot which put him in a long term medical facility flat on his back for several months. During his period of in-activity, he taught himself how to make flowers out of paper napkins with the aid of a craft book. Kept him from going crazy he told me. Thanking him again for the white rose, I started to enter my vehicle when he again said, "That is really a nice car." I dismissed my non-verb "OOPS" immediately and turned to face him, smiled and said to him, "Yeah, it is but its only something I bought. I can't make a white rose out of paper. Now that is really something." My smile stayed with me until my coffee cup was empty and I was asleep.

The next evening at work, I told some of my co-workers the story of my little adventure. I had no idea that before my shift was over that this story would become a tool for healing.

By 0230 hours, I was starting to count the hours until the end of shift. I was working a radio position that served three stations. The radio reliefs had just left for lunch. The shift had been uneventful but busy and I could feel the staff settle in for the long routine early morning hours. The dispatchers sitting in the immediate area of my console were now able to speak to each other in full sentences since the radio traffic had slowed to a reasonable pace.

The call that would send two deputies to a remote area of the county came in around 0300 hours. The suspect was the husband of the victim. The victim had been beaten and threatened by the suspect who had an M-1 rifle either in his possession or had access to it. No doubt this was a heads up call, but unfortunately, not that unusual. Primary unit, One Sam Thirty-five, was advised on the air of the circumstances and acknowledged receiving the call on the MDT. His back up, One Sam Twenty-five, also advised he was en route. One Sam Thirty-five requested a call be made back to the reporting party, a neighbor, to get an update and some further directions. I made the call from the console. I would hear and the RP would tell me that shots were being fired just prior to the two units arrival. The two deputies on the call were advised of the shots being fired and arrived at the location; a dark desert section of the county with mobile homes on somewhat large parcels of property, within moments of acknowledging that they had copied. They arrived together, requested emergency traffic, and went on foot knowing that two additional units were en route. The area was made darker by a low cloud cover and slight rain. It was very cold, I would find out later. Still on the line with the RP, he advised that another volley of shots had just been fired. The RP did not have a visual of the suspect or the deputies. Over the radio I advised the two units of the additional shots fired. The did not respond. The dispatchers in the Communications Center stopped talking even though they could not hear all that was being said. Someone asked what area. I told them, then added for my own comfort, that it was a bad HT area. I tried raising the units again. Again, no response. The Station Watch Commander, Sam One Ten, was already en route as well as another unit, One Charles Mary. I confirmed with Sam One Ten that he copied the negative response to the radio traffic. He had.

I toned the officers at the scene one at a time.

Negative response.

The RP still did not see the suspect or the deputies. The tension in the immediate area of my console grew palatable. The watch commander from a neighboring station would ask on the air of the responding watch commander if he needed additional units. The responding watch commander answered, "Not at this time. It's a bad radio area." I translated that to mean that the neighboring watch commander would get as close to the location as possible without going out of his station boundaries and secretly thanked Sam One Ten for confirming that the location was a known "bad radio" area. It allowed my body tension to go one click down on my alert scale. A K-9 unit not assigned to the handling station, and on his way home, came up on the radio advising that he was available if needed, from a location about 10-15 minutes from the scene. Having worked with this K-9 unit in the past, I knew he was going to start that way. I tried to raise the two deputies several more times. Negative response.

Time passed.

The RP still couldn't see anything. The suspect and the two deputies had vanished in the night. I could hear the constant crying of the suspect's wife in the background on the phone. My urge to have the RP tell her to *"shut the f..k up"* was almost overwhelming.

Time passed.

Tension grew.

The radio relief dispatchers returned from lunch talking to each other. No one had to say anything. They caught the mood of the room on their own. Michelle, the most senior of them looked at me and after being briefed by someone, asked if I wanted her to take the phone. I transferred the call to her console in front of me. This allowed me to focus only on radio traffic. I was grateful to her then, but later I would be overwhelmed by the way she stayed on the phone with the suspect's wife, changing forever her emotional matrix of the events. She would hold the common focus of the deputies safety in her mind, but interlaced with that was the tearful plea of a woman for her husband's safety.

Time passed.

The watch commander, Sam One Ten and his back up, One Charles Mary, arrived and were going in on foot. Sam One Ten advised that they had found the two units, but not the deputies.

Time passed.

I was breathing through my skin so that the noise of my breath could not be heard in my ears.

Time passed.

Einstein was right. It is all relative.

I reached out for the talk key to check on the newest units at the scene. The radio screen lit with the HT number of what was One Charles Mary, the watch commander's back up unit. It only indicated that he was trying to get a transmission out. We, (nearly every dispatcher on the side of the room was listening), could not copy any of the transmission.

Keying slowly, speaking clearly, I advised the unit that we could not copy any of his transmission. Then it came. I heard with my whole body, not just my ears, "11-99," officer down.

Time stopped.

Nerves that I never knew existed raced through my body to my ears, heating me and stopping my heart motion all at once. My hands shook. I stood up and repeated over the air, "11-99" and the address.

My voice cracked when I came to the "ninety-nine" portion of the code. I violated, on my highest codes of dispatching; "Keep the deputies tethered to you with voice tones." Letting them know that I am very present for them and that the situation and its implications are known to me, that I am in control and prepared to do whatever is necessary. It tells them that they are not alone or forgotten. My cracking of my voice was testament to my failure to control my safe, little self. A new wave of heat born of shame passed through me and was gone as I keyed the radio to confirm units responding.

At that moment, all the clocks on the walls would have two faces; one full of activity and tension marking the moments in precision; the other, without hands that brought us all to a place where events blend together and become scared.

The next four hours would bring officers from many agencies, special equipment, paramedics at risk to their own safety, commanders, captains, and the press to the scene. It would bring to my console, coffee and water, an off duty dispatcher to sit next to me just because; my station captain just in case, and thousands of inquiries from people in the dispatch center daring to take their attention off the events to inquire about my needs.

By 0700 hours, the citizens involved in the incident were safely out of the area. The suspect was still outstanding. The watch commander and his back up, One Charles Mary, after four hours of laying next to the fallen deputies, were somewhere on the outside of the perimeter. The original responding deputies were still laying in the spot where they fell. The coroner would bare them gently home for us.

By 0710, the new shift of dispatchers came into the radio room to relieve us. They entered silently, crushed by the briefing news they had just received. I would remain at my console with a sense that the suspect would be located soon. Most of the night shift would reluctantly go to the briefing room as instructed by the captain.

Around 0800 hours, the suspect stepped out from an open field. The Emergency Services Teams (SWAT), took him into custody unharmed. I said, "Copy, one in custody." I looked up at Barbara, a friend and dispatcher, who had just arrived for the day shift and was sitting next to me. "I'm leaving," I said. I stood and unplugged my headset and with legs that didn't seem to belong to me, walked out of the radio room.

The simplest of tasks were the only things I could focus on. *"I need to sign out. Sign out sheet is in the briefing room. I will go to the briefing room."* Coming to the doorway of the briefing room, I saw my fellow dispatchers sitting around a large table. I was confused momentarily by this and when I couldn't come up with a reason for being there, I dismissed it.

I was now mechanically thinking, *"Go to the sign out sheet. Sign your name."* Robotically, I went to the sign out sheet noticing a woman dressed in civilian clothes at the head of the table. I started to wonder who she was, but the effort was too much, so I dismissed her and went back to my task. "Sign the sheet, then you get to go home." Looking down at the sign out sheet, in a moment of revelation, I realized why everyone was in the room. They were waiting to find out about the suspect and there I was with the information and to self-involved to tell them. *"I should tell them,"* was my next thought. Looking sideways with my head still down I said, "The suspect is in custody." I hit a feeling and spit out the rest of the information, "He is unharmed." No one in the room reacted. My thoughts coming from a childlike area of my brain, *"I'm allowed to go home now. They can't make me stay."* I left the room.

Exiting the briefing room, I nearly ran into the office manager in the hallway. She looked at me, seemingly embarrassed by saying with a reserved smile, "How are you today?" I realized she had no idea how to handle this situation. My mind kicked up a few gears and silently voiced an *"I-have-definitely-got-to-get-out-of-here"* warning before I say what I really think of her practical inquiry.

I walked outside into the daylight.

The sun hit my face and suddenly my mind was an adult again, albeit, an indecisive one.

I wanted to go home, but first I needed to know that all the dispatchers that worked the incident and bore the burden with me, were all right. I wanted them to know I was Okay.

It seemed possible, in that moment of sun light, that this had all been a bad mistake. Maybe I had been dreaming awake. If I waited and willed and believed it hard enough that someone would come out in the sunlight and tell me that the two deputies were alive. For a moment so short, even scientists with their computer driven machines couldn't measure it, with the disparity of the sunlight and knowledge of what had occurred inside that building, I believed it might be possible to reel back time so I could warn them, or hide the call, or do anything so that they would be safe. I could get the other dispatchers to help. I knew they would. We could reel back time, change the ending, make it right. The image vanished as if it had not existed. I felt I had missed an undiscovered opportunity. I failed again to keep them safe. My parental mind raised its silent head with, *"Stop it! That is magically thinking. It can happen under stress, but does no good. No good at all. Get a grip."* "I'm sorry," I said out loud to myself.

I found myself sitting in the gazebo just outside the exit door to the Communications Center. Several other dispatchers were sitting there too. I felt numb and the moment seemed surreal. *"You need to be strong.,"* was my mantra for the moment. I was sitting next to Donna, a dispatcher I had worked with for about 3 years. She put her arms around me and said the most extraordinary thing, "You have always been here for us. You have listened to our problems and now it is time for us to be here for you." I thought she had me confused with someone else, but she was so sincere that her words went right past my logic and straight to my heart. I cried on her shoulder. Other dispatchers would join us. We talked how unbelievable it was. We talked about some of the things that happened. We sat for periods of time in silence. We wondered if the families had been told.

Michelle, the dispatcher who offered and took the phone line that the suspect's wife was on and spent hours talking to her, walked out of the center with her best friend. She was going to the parking lot. I called her by name. I wanted to thank her. I hugged her. We cried. She left. People seemed to wander in and out of the gazebo, stunned, disbelieving, wanting to do something, just anything to help each other. The station captain artfully came out a few times. No doubt to check on us. On one of his trips, he offered to have someone drive me home. The offer was so sweet that it almost surpassed a brief feeling of fear that my car, that freedom machine, would not be available to me. I had to have my flight mobile. No way someone would drive me home. I needed control of something. I simply told him I was fine to drive home.

The woman who had been sitting at the head of the table in the briefing room was now out in the gazebo with us. Someone had told me that she was from our agency's contract psychiatric services and had been called in to "handle" the emotional trauma that we might be experiencing. Katie, a stunning young woman, a good friend and one of the closest dispatchers to the action, had been crying so hard, I went over and put my arms around her. We talked, forehead to forehead, when I noticed that she still looked good...you know, no red eyes or running nose. I pointed out to her that she could have at least have the common courtesy to have a running nose. I jokingly asked her how she managed to cry without looking bad. We both laughed and cried at the same time. The woman in the civilian clothes, already an outsider, began a short commentary on how healthy this type of sharing was. I heard but didn't feel her remarks and continued my time with Katie. I filed her remark under my "I'll be pissed off about his one later" file.

The 35 minute trip to my home would take me one hour. My normal freeway cruising speed of 75 mph was reduced to 45 mph behind an obviously un-smogged truck that leaned to one side. Alone for the first time, I felt like a sheet of glass rested between me and the rest of the world. Watching the "public" drive down the road reminded me of an old video game my sons played, Pacman. They traveled down life's road just munching whatever is in front of them. I didn't consider this a judgment. Just a fact. I could see them around the TV later in the day watching the news. The third lead would be about the shooting and the arrest of the suspect. I saw a man who made no comment to his wife about the story, but simply asked her to pass the potatoes as he shoveled meat loaf into his mouth. This incident would be just another story on the news for them. The two families that had been forever changed would not enter their minds. The two men who would never again play ball with their children, make mistakes, argue and make love to their wives, or grow old and have the last voice they hear be someone's they loved and knew, did not enter into "these" people's hearts. They were not worth it. My unfocused anger was like a cold blade that cut me off from the people I had served and I was ashamed.

I was finally home. It felt like I had been gone for weeks. I went upstairs and took a bath so I could relax. The bath took under 5 seconds. I could not sit still. I paced. My dog paced. I went downstairs. Laid down on the couch. Got up. Sat in the chair.

Decided that I needed to do something physical. Pondered going to pick up a brass bed frame from a store one block away from my house. Decided that was an excellent plan even though I didn't own a truck to transport it. The solution was simple. I would carry the brass bed frame home from the store a piece at a time. This was actually better than going in a truck to pick it up. It would allow me to burn off some no longer needed energy. The distance was long enough and the location busy enough that someone was bound to do something funny when they saw me carrying the brass bed frame down the street. The big plus was that I could set up my new bed. I had done enough odd things frequently enough that no one would think anything of it, I reasoned. One problem arose that stalled my plan. I couldn't make up my mind which pair of shoes to wear for my adventure. I asked my dog. He was resting exhausted from the pacing and offered no opinion. I ran another bath to consider my options. Stayed in the tub for a good minute this time. Called a friend, Susan from work, knowing she was on her days off. She had not heard the news. I told her and it became more real for me in the telling. She was coming over and bringing a mutual friend of ours, a deputy with her. She told me to wait on the bed frame, they would bring a truck. I dressed in my other uniform, blue jeans and a sweat shirt and was able to select a pair of shoes.

While I waited for Susan and Kelly to arrive, I went over the details of the incident. Questioned myself without mercy and from out of no where, a cold thought hit me. I couldn't remember where I had put my headset. I had to have someone look for it. I called work and asked a friend of mine, Barbara, to find it for me. I couldn't believe I was so careless to leave it somewhere. I confessed to her that I was in a bit of a panic about it and requested she call me back.

I headed downstairs when the phone started ringing. I went to pick it up and absent mindedly picked up the white paper rose that had been made for me the night before. It was Barbara calling from work. She wanted to let me know that my headset was found in my locker where I had put it. She added that the captain had heard about my concern and said he felt sure they could find me another headset if mine wasn't located. We both thought that was funny since there were no extra headsets in the whole of the communications center. We hung up. I still had the white rose in my hand.

There were a lot of phone calls from co-workers and friends. I would answer their questions. They would give me updates. Barbara called back to tell me that the color guards were not with the two deputies. She wisely thought I would want to know. *"Yes, oh yes Barbara, I'm glad you called. That helps. They are not alone. They have someone to watch over them."* It felt like I had finally gotten off duty.

Susan and Kelly arrived. The phone rang again. Kelly, a K-9 officer at a different station than the one where the incident occurred, was petting my dog as I answered the phone. It was Bob, the call taker who had generated the original call. We talked for a while about what happened. Then his courageous question came and I knew what it meant to him. "Why did you call back the RP?" The question came hard for him as it would anyone in that position. I told him the truth, the deputies wanted an update and some very detailed directions. The call was perfect. We talked some more. I told him in detail what had transpired. I was watching Kelly's reaction to the conversation. She was witnessing first hand how dispatchers cared and how our lives are interwoven with the deputies in the field. I hung up with Bob, proud that I knew him because he had the kind of character that allowed him to make the call and grateful that he saw me as the kind of person he could call.

Susan and Kelly and I took a breath and then decided it was time to go retrieve my new brass bed frame from the store. We arrived at the store only to find it was closed. Kelly, not dissuaded and in true cop fashion, got out of the truck and started investigating the possibility that someone might be inside the store. She pounded on the front door, shook it, put her nose against the glass. Susan and I were in the truck laughing our heads off as well as placing bets on how long it would take her to give up on our failed adventure. It seemed strange and wonderful to laugh.

I arrived home a few minutes later with messages on my answer machine and the phone ringing. The on duty supervisor called to tell me I could have the night off. He said he doubted I had slept. I would return the calls.

That evening seven of the dispatchers from the incident would make the long trip to my house so we could go out for a while. We sat in a bar, not drinking, but discussing the newest information related to the call. Bob had joined us late, having already returned to work and when he asked to be relieved, the request was denied. With ample dispatchers on duty, he left. We bitched about supervision making such a decision and were proud of Bob for walking out.

The sports bar we selected had several TV's running at the same time on two different channels. The TV that I saw most easily was showing a football game already played. The other channel was a news broadcast with a camera shot, that from my peripheral vision, had all primary color. The blue of sky, bright yellow crime scene tape, green bushes and a number of black and whites parked in the area. The lead story had film of the crime scene shot in the daylight hours, feeding the public's "right" to know. A wave of disgust rolled over me. The county newspaper had already done damage in the holy name of journalism by printing a face up picture of one of the dead deputies on the front page.

Later, the newspaper would run an article defending its action by saying that it was their responsibility to educate the public on the results of domestic violence and taking the high moral ground, when some of the public responded to their action, the editor would wonder why we weren't discussing the issues of family violence and its causes instead of being offended by a picture depicting the outcome of the violence. Discussion! They wanted to discuss it when the deputies they so cavalierly dismissed by printing one of their photos hadn't discussed it. They showed up and it cost them their lives, not for day, but forever. It didn't stop there, it cost four young children from really knowing their fathers.

The visualization that served me well as a dispatcher, my method of tracking the deputies and their activities, becomes an enemy to me in that moment. I saw an off duty deputy's intent stride going to the front of a newly widowed woman's house to retrieve the newspaper with the picture of her dead husband. I was in silent rage.

All the dispatchers sitting at the table were acutely aware of the TV coverage and, wounded themselves, tried to protect me. Suddenly, Katie got up and walked up to the bartender and asked him to turn the channel. He complied with the request only after she gave him an explanation.

Someone had brought me a teddy bear, a gift from another dispatcher. The gift selected was for me because I often carried a teddy bear named Stanley to work. Stanley's greatest attribute is his huggability. He had suffered kidnapping at the hands of my fellow dispatchers, several ransom notes were delivered to me and he was eventually located in the captain's office. He was often called upon just to sit next to a dispatcher during stressful moments. He became part of the shifts I worked and was available to anyone who may need him. This new teddy bear came to me that night with a hope he might comfort me. He came unnamed. Everyone at the table offered several possible names for the newest member of the shift. None seemed suitable. Finally, Katie came up with a name that was a combination of the two fallen deputy's last names. We christened him that night and later he would have a name tag like Stanley's to wear. I never carried him to work.

I watched and participated in this process going on between all of us at the table. I knew this was part of the healing process. I had hoped, knowing that would make the process easier. It made it identifiable and so I gained a margin of control. I wondered if I was a low level coward, afraid to feel and experience all that had happened.

I paced that night for several hours and finally slept for two hours.

My son, Christopher, called the next morning. He was on his way over to take me to lunch. In the restaurant I told him in outline form what had happened. Then, he reached across the table and held my hand, "Mom," he asked, "what would make you feel better?" I told him I wanted to do something for the dispatchers on my shift. They had all shown up so completely for the deputies and me. It needed to be something special. Then it came to me. A white rose. No, two white roses for each of them. We were on our way to search out every white rose available in the town.

Going back to work that night, the front seat of my car was filled with white roses. The briefing room was my first trip on my journey back. The line up was read. When my name was called, I was scheduled to work the same position that I was at some 30 hours before. I froze. It seemed I was required to go back to what was for me, in essence, the crime of the scene. For the first time in my tenure with the department, I refused a direct order. The supervisor, realizing the oversight, generously reassigned me to a phone position after my co-workers offered to trade the tainted radio position for the positions assigned to them.

I spent the shift on phones being curt with the public and leaving white roses on the consoles of my co-workers. It was a long night and I realized I was both watched and watched over. I took it as a threat and a kindness. I had seen department management indirectly make it nearly impossible for anyone displaying any kind of emotion or individualism, to continue to work. This process is justified by stating over and over again, it is for the "good of the department." It is their mantra and their holy grail. We, the workers, were expected and all too often, believed that there was such a thing as "the department" aside from the people and the services we provided. The fear based belief, which directed them, had been established over years of cutting off their own humanity, not to provide a service, but to be seen as someone who can "take it." To "take it" only required you to control with impunity, your own feelings. Yes, we could morn as long as we did it within the framework of what was proper and don't ask too many questions. Their concern was, could the person produce. I was being watched, but no more than I was watching myself.

I was also being watched over. It is an amazing feeling to be watched over. It brings with it a gentle strength. The shift would end and I would begin to wonder if I could still do the job. I reviewed the incident again. I had no answer.

Two funerals in two days. They blend in my memory. Flashing lights on the top of patrol units in a single line for as far as the eye could see; flagged draped coffins, fly by's with helicopters, hugs, tears, the long drive down a desert street with Boy Scouts holding their hands over their hearts and an old woman standing by a mailbox holding a sign that expressed her sorrow as the processional passed; the blue sky resting on a brown desert floor, church pews packed to capacity with people standing against the walls, and speaking to the women who had lost their life partner to an assassin's anger. All of these hold a place in my heart's memory, but the clearest of all memories would be the gathering of warriors in a parking lot of a mall; the staging point for the final funeral procession.

That day, the dispatchers going to the funeral met at the communications center where we were to travel in marked units to the staging point. A dispatcher that was going to the services came up to me, clearly upset, and informed me that she had been told that we were not to wear our angel pins, that had been made for us, on our uniforms. The angles began as a way for Barbara to do something for the shift that was on duty that night. The project gave Barbara something to do immediately after the incident. She decided to make two angel pins for me and place a white rose in the angles hands. One of the pins given to me was donated by a training supervisor; a gift to her from a grateful trainee. Each dispatcher that worked that night would be given a pin, as well as the widows. The idea took on a life of its own. People throughout the department requested one of the pins and the project was finally taken over by the staff at the jail. The pins were made and the contributions given to the families of the fallen officers. The dispatcher that told me we could not wear the pin didn't know who had given the order prohibiting us from placing them on our lapel. The politics of this day did not fall into the realm of the important for me. The solution seemed simple to me. Let the person who issued the order take the two pins off my uniform. No one did. We all wore the pins. I never found out if such an order had been issued.

The lieutenant who was in charge of arranging the transportation units we were to take to the staging point, in true passive-aggressive style, was not yet in uniform when it was time to leave. The units were lined up in a neat little row in the parking lot. His car was the lead car. Several dispatchers were asking when we were going to leave. I asked the captain the same question. He was waiting for the lieutenant that, as he put it, was always late. I said we were going without him. My co-workers were stressing because they did not want to be late, and so was I. We backed up all the marked units from the lead car and headed for the staging area. We discussed the possibility of getting reprimanded for the move on the way to the staging point. It didn't much matter, we knew from some place deep inside, that we couldn't treat this a business as usual. We were going to a gathering of warriors to say we're sorry and to bid one more of them goodbye.

We arrived to find a parking lot full of marked units from our agency as well as other agencies. Men and women dressed in Class A's were standing near the units in small groups. Their faces told a story of disbelief and sorrow. I would be introduced to several deputies that I had worked with and had never met in person. We talked in hush voices, heads dropping down when the words came hard. Deputies that I had met over the years would place their arms around me and I would do the same. Here, a ritual was taking place, without design, a map or order from the top. Here among the people who serve and do the job everyday. It is a secret ritual.

The trip to the community where the second officer was buried would bring several more marked units into the processional, until all that you could see was the red, blue and amber lights in both directions. Sitting in the church next to Michelle, I could hear her crying. We held hands. On my left sat a Sergeant who was a long time friend. He pointed out a small tree on the piece of paper that listed information about the deputy whose service we were attending. It reminded him of a place that was special to him. He would look down at it several times and gently touch it with his finger. Sitting two people over, Sally was crying uncontrollably in her mother's arms. I would sit through the service nearly dry eyed. When the service concluded, we made the trip back to the communications center in silence.

Arriving at the comm center, the day to day business of emergency services hit us in the face like cold water. The shift I worked on was scheduled to work that night. Two days of attending funerals and it was back to work for most of the people who had just left the grave site. I went home exhausted.

I asked for and was granted a weeks vacation. We all needed a break.

That week brought a flood of phone calls from deputies, dispatchers, and friends. Some would call and cry, then say goodbye, others would talk about problems they were experiencing at home, and all would ask how I was doing.

How was I doing? My body was still in a rage for peace. I had so much nervous energy that I could not sit still and at the same time, I was aching for sleep. I went to the gym for two hours in the morning and one hour at night. Those times of exercise, I would bring up an emotion and work the sets until it burned away. Between the gym, I worked in my little garden, cleaned closets, color coded my clothing in my dresser, walked my dog, talked to normal people in my neighborhood, and conducted Monday Morning Quarter backing of my actions during the incident. I made lists of things to do and didn't get them done. I paced. I slept with dreams that broke my heart. I returned to work ready to resume my normal schedule. Whatever emotional residue that remained would take care of itself over time.

A few weeks had passed. I was sleeping as normally as you can working an early morning shift. My co-workers were still running on nervous to hyper vigilant; so was I. The work kept us busy and occupied.

One night working the console where the incident occurred, the phone rang. It was Sergeant Jones, the man who had stayed on the ground next to his deputy. I had met him and his wife briefly at one of the funerals and he had generously called me at home soon after the incident. He had heard my voice over the radio and called to say hello. We chatted and during the conversation, he made an offer to take me to the scene of the incident. Several of the dispatchers had made the trip out to the location. I had not. I told him I would call him when I was ready to make the trip. He understood.

We made the trip a few days later. He selected an unmarked unit because, as he put it, "There had been enough black and whites in that area over the past few weeks." He mentioned to me that he was surprised that I came out that night. I said I wanted to see the location as close to how it looked that night, if possible. He drove the several miles from the station to the scene, noting different landmarks in the station boundaries as we traveled down the freeway.

He parked the unit in the same spot where he had parked the unit the night of the incident. He pointed out where the original responding units had parked and what they had done in the last moments of their lives. There, at that moment, I caught the intensity of their approach. Two men in the dark working in tandem, coming up to a place of rage. Focused and acutely aware of the world around them. Struck down in the midst of the intensity of the work they had chosen. This was a sacred place.

Sergeant Jones took me to the area where the suspect hid and where he placed the weapon. Jones would also remark on how much the weather was the same as it was in the early morning hours several weeks earlier. It was overcast with a slight bit of rain. It was very cold, he told me. I could see how this brought him back to those moments with a stunning, silent blow, and I stood in awe of the kind of courage he displayed. Not just the incident where he spent hours next to the bodies of two men whom he worked with and supervised, but for walking me through the incident. I couldn't even imagine the kind of sorrow that he was feeling.

The days would pass. I would, on occasion, have moments where the feelings of the incident would sweep over me without warning. I could keep myself under control by swallowing hard, taking deep breaths and continue working. They came less often as the days passed. I was fine.

Jerry, a dispatch supervisor on temporary assignment to a different station, came into the comm center to work an overtime shift in early February. I ran into him outside the center and we talked briefly. He told me he had recently attended a class in critical incident stress management and debriefing. It had brought up several things he had not dealt with in a fatal shooting of a deputy that he handled twelve years earlier. He wanted me to go to the class and made the arrangement.

The class was on Valentine's Day. Jerry had managed to get me a comp seat and I had traded a day with a fellow dispatcher so that I could attend.

Walking down the hall to the class, I was greeted by a man who introduced himself as Richard Behr. He said that Jerry had told him to look after me. My heart sank. I had hoped to be just another dispatcher attending a class, not the one that "handled the call where two officers were killed." My cover was already blown.

I entered the classroom reluctant to give up my anonymity. I selected a seat on the right side of the room, second row. I based my selection on the fact that most people are right handed. Guessing the speaker would be right handed and therefore, favor her right side both visually and physically, I placed myself on what would be the speaker's left side, close but not too close, to the front of the class and not so far back that her wide range of vision would pick me up. This is my grown up variation on the method I used as a child for keeping the Boogie Man from getting me in the night. I simply made myself invisible in my bed by lying still and melting into the sheets. This childhood practice always worked because I had never once been found by the Boogie Man. The proof of this was evident to me by my presence in the room, second row far to the left.

The class, comprised of dispatchers from surrounding agencies, began to take their seats while I was tucked safely into my little spot. Then Christa, a dispatcher from my agency, who had been working in another assignment away from the center, entered the room and sat down next to me. Christa didn't know it, but she was just about to become my momentary designated dump site for anger. My throat tightened and my thoughts went to "if only." *If only I had gotten that temporary position away from the center instead of her. If only that would have happened, she would be the one sitting here trying to look like it was business as usual. Besides, everyone knew she got the position based upon favoritism, not ability.* "You're a real bitch," talking about myself. "Fuck it! It's true," I responded back. I, of course, turned to her and smiled asking how she was doing. We chatted.

I wondered why she was here and not some of the other dispatchers who had worked the incident that night, and besides, she was getting paid for attending the class. I was on my own time. Her kids and husband were doing well. I admonished myself for my nasty thoughts. I would not wish these circumstances on any dispatcher...although I just had. *"Let it go. Sit back under the cover*

*of the seating plan and try and learn something. You owe it to Jerry.
He went to a lot of trouble to get you into the class."*

Janet Childs was introduced by the Chief of Police of the host
agency. Janet entered from the back of the room. Slight built,
wearing a red power dress and carrying a guitar. *"This is going to
be interesting,"* I thought.

Janet did the traditional opening giving her professional history
and defining what Critical Incident Stress Management and Debriefing was and how it developed. Then came the moment where
the speaker has each class member introduce themselves and, in
this case, tell about an incident in their career that has left its mark.
She started at the back of the room. I wanted to hear the other
dispatchers stories, but my goal not to be identified as the one who
handled "that call," was still my top priority. I decided to pick
another one; one that wasn't so big. I had plenty to select from; the
fourteen year old that had fatally shot his friend in the chest, the
invalid man who was burned alive in a fire with his wife being held
back by a deputy and her screams that came over the radio as the
deputy called for help, the woman who found her friend dead with
the victim's three year old locked inside the home...there were plenty
of others. I would just pick one when my turn came.

I sat listening to dispatchers talk. I was so focused on what they
were saying that I didn't notice that the next person to speak was
my momentarily designated dump site for anger, the dispatcher
from my agency sitting next to me. She began by saying her name
and our agency name, where she was assigned and then...it came.
She calmly stated, "Well, my incident isn't nearly as awful as the
shooting of the two deputies that she handled last month..." She
had turned and pointed to me with her head. It was an "Aw shit"
moment for me. She had blown my plan. I was stuck. Not only that,
my clever selection of seating was now working against me. I would
have to turn in my seat to speak to the class since no one was sitting
in the front row. Embarrassed, that I couldn't even control my seat
selection, I tried telling myself the be calm. That I could control.
My designated dump site continued to talk as I calmed myself. I
have no idea what she said.

I was up to bat but my thought process had gone south. Janet
saved me briefly with a few words. I turned and looked at the other
dispatchers. They had questions. They were hurting for all of us
that had lost these men. They had lost them, too. These dispatchers
became a different kind of extended family. I felt small for trying
to hide from them.

They told me where they were that night. How they pulled up
our frequency to listen. They told me I did a good job. They talked
about the offer to voluntarily work at my agency's center so that our

dispatchers could attend the funerals. An offer that was unfortunately refused.

Janet would say it for me during the class. What I wanted most. She said it quietly, softly but with truth that brings your heart to its knees. What did I want most? I wanted them back! These men I didn't know. I wanted them with their families, I wanted them to feel the sunlight on their faces, to watch and direct their children's growth, to make mistakes and good decisions, to experience the wonder of life. I wanted them back. That was my ground zero.

Janet would take us through the class with humor, tears and the skill of an emotional mine sweeper. That day was good. I had met some courageous people who were not afraid to explore the emotional grit of the work done everyday in emergency services.

Three years have passed over me since those times. I have enjoyed working with Richard Behr and people like him, establishing a CISD team for Southern California. The efforts are slow, but I have already seen them bare fruit. I have seen and been a part of the positive effects of CISD debriefings. I believe that to heal, you must have a safe place to admit that you are wounded; people who have some knowledge and experience in the situations emergency services personnel deal with on a day to day basis to assist you, and people around you that experienced the incident with you-field personnel and dispatchers alike. I believe now as I did when I hired onto the sheriff's department, that the real challenge for me would be to find a balance between the control of the job and the effects the work has on your heart. That balance can never be struck by failing to acknowledge one in order to pretend you have the other.

I was very lucky. I had wonderful people around me; dispatchers, deputies, watch commanders, supervisors, and captains. I have had occasions to speak to many different emergency professionals over the three years. The oddest thing would happen when I would be talking to them, one on one. They would tell me their story. No matter the rank of the person, no matter the level of support they have for the concept of CISD, they would tell me one of their stories. Each story would come to me as a gift of trust and realization of how well I was treated. No, supervision did not do all they could for the dispatchers that were involved in my incident, but I know they tried. They may not have done it just the way it should have been done, if there is such a thing, but they did try...at least most of them did. They had their own pain to deal with; old war wounds that were never attended to and for the most part they had no idea what to do. No matter how many times we say "this is part of the job," the reality of it is easy to ignore in order to "do the job." Left unattended, these wounds cause the death of careers and of people.

I spent most of my energy in those days trying to feel normal and, most importantly, look normal because "this is part of the job." This is what we get paid to do. My best wish for people in law enforcement is that they put down this myth. Certainly, it does happen, but when we try to minimize its cost, we devalue ourselves, the work and life itself. It's hard to see the difference between being tough and strong, especially in the middle of one of life's storms. It is one of the foremost challenges of the work.

Three years later, I am no longer in law enforcement. I miss it. Mostly I miss the people, the action and the sense of contributing I always received from the work. I still work on CISD programs and believe that it's concepts are a good beginning.

There are times when memories of that night sweep over me. It comes all at once without a lot of detail. When this happens, my heart is soothed by the wave of caring that was shown to me and I'm overwhelmed with the odd way life has presented its gift to me. Do I still want the deputies back? Certainly, I do. But I also know they will never be lost to me in the darkness of that desert night. I carry them with me. They are white roses that I can now keep in my heart. Because of the helping hearts of my colleagues, the support of CISD members, family and friends, I carry them with me. This...is no burden.

Texas A&M Tragedy

I just made it in from the game. I'm so tired. Here is the letter of my experience at the bonfire for you. I went to a mandatory stress relief council this morning with my fellow Texas A&M University Police and Security Officers. I was told the best way to cope with what we experienced is to talk about it. So, to all my friends, I'd like to share with you step by step November 18, 1999.

I was awakened approximately 10 minutes after the fall. I arrived on scene at 3:30am. It was shocking. I walked up to the command post with new batteries for other officers. They told me to walk around and give them out to all who needed them. It was then that I walked toward the bonfire. As I approached, I could hear the screams of pain. People still visible in the stack. Some alive, others gone. Medical personnel working on the injured, logs being surgically cut by firefighters to rescue and remove the deceased. Students wanting to help, getting through the police tape and trying to help but getting in the way. Some were authorized to stay. One I spoke to. He told me he just heard a loud SNAP! and it just fell right over. I asked how many were in the stack still? He estimated at least thirty. Then he got choked up. I put my hand on his shoulder and he walked away sobbing.

Several students broke through the line on the east side. We rushed there and stopped them. They begged us to let them help. What could they do? It was then that a small number with pots (hard hats) were given the task to haul off logs removed by rescuers. I then went to the far east side to secure that sector. This was where the bonfire actually fell. This would be where I would remain. I stood there with some students watching as I was. More pots would arrive and try to assist. It was now about 4:30am and construction pieces were continuously arriving. I was asking, "How did it arrive so fast?" Then Lowes came with a truck full of lumber. This was less than two hours after it fell and in the middle of the night. How did Lowes know? And all of this equipment and materials were donated. They didn't ask if they needed them, they just came with them.

The lumber would later be constructed to form support for the logs to prevent the structure from further falling. An older man, sixty years, approached me. He asked, "How many?" I told him I had no numbers (at that time it was six dead, nine still inside). I asked if he was a family member. He said, "No, just an old ag." He then walked among the students. It was then that I shed my first of many tears.

5:15am. The first helicopter from Houston arrives circling overhead. I then realized, "My God, this is going to be on national news. This is really big." I never new just how much media until later.

The first sings of day light approached. I was relieved to go use the restroom and get a drink. Food services had a buffet already established. Tents from Pop Abilities were set up. And McDonalds was sending bag after bag of food over to us. I walked by the morgue which was a College Station fire truck parked next to a trailer with sheets spread out for a door. There the bodies lay. Four at that time. Two yet to be pulled out and nine still inside unknown.

By daybreak the students had all moved to my section for the best view. All the pots stood by here. When needed, a senior would come and grab a number of them to relieve others. They continued to remove the logs away from the rescue effort as they were lifted off by crane. We didn't want all the pots inside the perimeter at once because they would get in the way. I was told a couple of days ago by two band members that us allowing them to help out like that, was the best therapy for them. I knew this to be true just looking at the helpless look on their faces.

A female student came walking up to me. She held a bag and handed it out to me and asked if I needed anything to eat. I smiled and replied, "No, thank you." She smiled back and continued on her way. Det. Villereal called me on the radio and told me to stop her and send her to him. He was a few yards away walking toward me. I stopped her and sent her to him. He talked to her and wrote down some info on a tablet. She walked back to me and I asked (in a jokingly manner), "Are you in trouble?" She smiled and said no. Then her face went serious. "My baby sister was working on the bonfire when it fell and I have yet to find her so I am just keeping busy."

My heart went out to her, so helpless she was. I told her I would pray for her and pray I did. A few minutes later, she came back by holding a pot. She asked if she could go inside to ask her Aggie brothers and sisters if they had seen her. I told her, "Put your pot on and go help out removing those logs. Leave your bag with me." She gathered such a smile, put on her pot and ran inside to help. Later, she came back to me and said they had someone at the hospital matching her description. She was smiling ear to ear and ran for her car. I never knew her name, or if her sister was Miranda or Jamie.

Three A&M busses arrived. They parked and formed a triangle. Sheets were placed on the opening between the busses and the new morgue was formed. The first of the hearses arrived and took away the bodies by the fire truck. The bodies were placed inside the busses where photographs and identification was done. The officers assigned to this took this very hard afterward.

A State Trooper arrived. He told me he needed to see President Bowen with a message from Governor Bush. It also contained the authorization of the Texas National Guard.

Just before 8am, a survivor was pulled out. An hour later, a second. One of these was the twelfth victim. All pots then moved back to me. They just sat down just inside the yellow police tape. I wasn't about to tell them to move behind the line. They all sat there, exhausted. I now had between five hundred and one thousand students and on lookers on my line. I met a lot of them. We were one.

A message came over our radios. "The fire department will now begin using listening devices to detect heartbeats, breathing and moaning. Have everyone be as quiet as possible. At this time, turn off your radios. We will tell you when it is over." And so I started from the south side of my line and told a small group what was going to happen and to pass it to your fellow Aggies behind you. I told six different sections this. On that sixth section, the last of the news helicopters was flying away to the airport.

I then looked at my students. They were all seated, looking outward at the accident site, and not one single person, nearly one thousand, was saying a word. I couldn't stand, I almost collapsed and fell to my knees at the site. I sat down, legs folded and a student put his arm on my shoulder embracing me. There I sat there among them. I was one of them watching and waiting for the next forty-five minutes.

I walked away with my Sergeant and good friend, Jack Rissmiller. I saw all the media. All the donations from Red Lobster, Outback Steakhouse, Golden Corral, On the Border, and so many others.

The organization, response and cooperation between the fire and rescue teams was outstanding. It was as if God was guiding them all and showing them exactly what to do. It was as if they had prepared for this for years, yet no one ever expected it. Not like this. What was seen on TV can never compare to what is really there. I know this now. Oklahoma City, earthquakes, etc. These images are only a small portion of the whole picture.

There is much I left out. I will never forget this or those twelve victims. A community brought together. I thank you for allowing me to share this with you. Talking about it helps a lot and gives you more of a better understanding. God Bless.

Mike Guidry, Security Officer
Texas A&M Police Department

(Officer Guidry was kind enough to allow his letter to be published in this book. Only grammatical changes were made. His words remain as he intended them...his feelings. His letter is a perfect example of getting those emotions to the surface where they are easily dealt with. Thanks go out to Officer Guidry for sharing his experience during the tragic event at Texas A&M.)

Taking Care of Yourself

An Apocryphal Tale

(I heard this several years back, but found it a few years ago on a web site)

I awoke early, as I often did, just before sunrise, to walk by the ocean's edge and greet the new day. As I moved through the misty dawn, I focused on a faint, far away motion. I saw a youth, bending and reaching and flailing arms, dancing on the beach, no doubt in celebration of the perfect day soon to begin. As I approached, I sadly realized that the youth was not dancing to the bay, but rather bending to sift through the debris left by the night's tide, stopping now and then to pickup a starfish and then standing, to heave it back into the sea. I asked the youth the purpose of the effort. "The tide has washed the starfish onto the beach and they cannot return to the sea themselves," the youth replied. "When the sun rises, they will die, unless I throw them back into the sea." As the youth explained, I surveyed the vast expanse of the beach, stretching in both directions beyond eyesight. Starfish littered the shore in numbers beyond calculation. The hopelessness of the youth's plan became clear to me and I countered, "But there are more starfish on this beach than you can ever save before the sun is up. Surely you cannot expect to make a difference." The boy paused briefly to consider my words, bent to pick up a starfish and threw it as far as possible. Turning to me he simply said, "I made a difference to that one."

*Author unknown

In Closing

As dispatchers, we make a difference in peoples lives everyday. We make decisions that affect people in ways that, sometimes, they don't realize, let alone us making that realization. We take peoples stress and grief and carry it around with us with little or no outlet for release. The purpose of this book is to let you know that you don't have to carry around that burden. We have given you some ways to cope with stress, some techniques to help alleviate stress and some guidelines to help you help yourself. If it were possible to wave the magic wand and make the stresses of the job go away, our lives would be much more simple. The information given is a compilation of several sources. Put it in your "dispatcher toolbox" and use your tools often. Not every tool is going to work for every person and situation. It's up to you to utilize whatever tools gets the job done for you. Find out what works and what doesn't; search for other tools to use or invent your own tools. We may not be in control of the events that occur in our lives, but we can be in control of our reactions to those events. World renown author on the stress and grieving process, Elisabeth Kubler-Ross, has a wonderful quote that I think applies to dispatchers; "People are like stained-glass windows. They sparkle and shine when the light is out, but when the darkness sets in, their true beauty is revealed only if there is a light from within." We make a difference every day in other people's lives. Make a difference in yours and take care of you and keep that light within you bright when the outside appears dark.

WEB Sites of Interest

PSTC911.COM

Public Safety Training Consultants. A private training provider that specializes in dispatcher training for law enforcement and fire fighting. The company is owned by a dispatcher, and all of the instructors are dispatchers, with the exception of a grief counselor and two police psychologists. The author teaches dispatcher related stress classes through PSTC.

GEOCITIES.COM/~HALBROWN

Hal Brown is a Clinical Social Worker that specializes in law enforcement stress and Post Traumatic Stress Disorder. The site is an excellent resource and if you replace the wording from "police officer" and replace it with "dispatcher," the information is just as valuable. The site even has a section on "Humor" and a feature article every month devoted to law enforcement.

TRAUMA-PAGES.COM/INDEX.PHTML

David Baldwin is a psychologist. This site is another excellent resource for dispatchers. It is also geared towards police officers, but here again, insert the word "dispatcher" and you have some more valuable information. The site also has an internal search engine to search for specific information.

AAETS.ORG

The American Academy of Experts in Traumatic Stress. This is a multi-disciplinary organization dedicated to the victims of trauma; any type of trauma. There are a few articles on law enforcement stress in the "Publications" section. This site also has a search engine to search for members, occupations and specialties. You'll even find 3 dispatchers as members. The author is a member of the Academy and is a Board Certified Expert in Traumatic Stress, and a Board Certified Expert in Emergency Crisis Response.

POLICESTRESS.ORG/INDEX.HTM

Central Florida Police Stress Unit, Inc is a non-profit organization that is not affiliated with any law enforcement agency. The site has areas for signs and symptoms of stress, training courses, law enforcement suicide and many more topics. It's another good site for information.

GEOCITIES.COM/CAPITOLHILL/LOBBY/3082/

Mercury Critical Incident Stress Team. This site gives some good insight into Critical Incident Stress Management and Debriefing, coping techniques and skills, and some techniques for family and friends to help cope with stress.

ICISF.ORG

International Critical Incident Stress Foundation, Inc. This is the "father" of stress management for emergency services. It was started by Dr. Jeffrey Mitchell and is one of the premier sources for stress management.

ISLANDNET.COM/SARBC/CIS1.HTML

Search and Rescue Society of British Columbia. Nice site with a usenet-like discussion area. Information on CIS Syndrome and some good links.

THEGRID.NET/CAMERA-MAN.ART1.HTM

Mary Helen Madrid is a nurse who does grief and stress management. The site has some great self-asking questions for you when you are under stress or grief.

THECENTRE.ORG

The Centre For Living With Dying. A non-profit organization that deals with the effects of death, grieving and stress. Located in Northern California, they are the home base for the Bay Area Critical Incident Stress Debriefing Team. Wonderful programs.

MADDMOM.COM

A personal web page of a California dispatcher. There are some prayers for dispatchers and lots of inspirational writings. A wonderfully done site with some great backgrounds. And the dispatcher designs her own site and maintains it, as well.

MINDTOOLS.COM/SMPAGE.HTML This site is called "Mind Tools Book Store" and is a very good site. It starts off with an introduction to stress management, understanding stress, recognizing symptoms, techniques, etc. The site is in association with Amazon.com and recommends a book on stress.

JOBSTRESSHELP.COM

Job Stress Help On-Line Consultation. You can submit queries about job stress, but the drawback is that they charge for a query. The bright side is that they have a couple of articles that are free. One is about lifestyle and managing stress. There is also a free survey that you can take and describe the type of stress you have. You can even give a description of the type of job you have and it's stressors. You'll also find an area on quick ways to relieve job stress.

STRESSFREE.COM

Stress Free NET. Interesting site that has a stress audit you can take. Be prepared to spend a little time taking it as it has 238 questions.

GDAY-MATE.COM

Interesting site from the land down under; Australia. The site has a menu of several things to choose from, including what is stress?, a stress test, a life events rating scale, quit smoking, etc. There are also some photos taken around Australia by the owner of the site, John Townsend. It's like learning about stress and taking a virtual vacation at the same time.

OURTOWNUSA.NET/~HUTKS911

The site is owned by a dispatcher in Kansas. It is the unofficial site of his agency. It has a comprehensive area on Dispatcher Prayers and Inspirational Writing for Dispatchers. Bob was kind enough to allow me to use some of the prayers and writings in this book, as he has compiled them from dispatchers all over the country, and possibly the world. Check out all the prayers and writings he has to offer.

GRYEYES.COM

This site is owned by a dispatcher on the Central California coast line and is a great place to get away from it all (both site and locale). A comprehensive site for police and fire dispatchers with links to sites of both disciplines. A very cool place with a section entitled "Brethren and Sistren of the Headset" (names and e-mail addresses of dispatchers from around the world.), PSAP Postcards, APCO Conference photos, sound files, etc. (Now that Linda, the owner has read this, she is probably doing her world famous "Snoopy" dance).

SEAOX.COM/CISM/CISM/HTML

Nice site with a listing of publications regarding critical incident stress management. Also links to various CISD teams.

911STRESS.COM

The owner of this site is a fire dispatcher and author. Frank Holt has written numerous articles related to dispatcher stress and has an article on the site entitled "The Top 10 Things You Should Know About Dispatcher Stress."

Order Form

Your shipping address:

Name		
Agency		
Address		
City	State	Zip
Daytime telephone (with area code)	Internet E-Mail address (optional)	

Your order:

Please send me the following order:		QTY	Totals
Under the Headset: Surviving Dispatcher Stress	$ 29.95 each		$
Sales Tax	Add 7.5% Sales Tax for items shipped to California addresses		$
Shipping	$3.00 for the first book and $1.50 for each additional book.		$
TOTAL	Enclose check, money order, or purchase order payable in US funds to "Staggs Publishing"		$

Government Purchase Orders and Personal Checks are Accepted!
(Credit Card Orders are only taken on-line at http://www.staggspublishing.com)

Thank you! Please mail your orders to:

Staggs Publishing
P.O. Box 890069
Temecula, CA 92589-0069

Questions? Call (909)698-6028 or E-Mail orders@staggspublishing.com

These books have unconditional guarantees. If you are not satisfied with any book you may return it for a full refund at anytime.

Quantity discounts are available for agencies and educators on orders for 11 or more books. Write or contact the publisher at (909)698-6028 for further information.